# Better And Stronger Apart

Also by Dr. David E. Williams

Provincial Police Training in Britain: Continuity and Reform 1947-1985
Japan: Beyond the End of History
Japan and the Enemies of Open Political Science
Defending Japan's Pacific War: The Kyoto Philosophers and Post-White Power
The Left in the Shaping of Japanese Democracy (edited with Rikki Kersten)
The Philosophy of Japanese Wartime Resistance: A Reading, with Commentary, of the Complete Texts of the Kyoto School Discussions of 'The Standpoint of World History and Japan'
Before We Go to War with China and North Korea
Brexit et après: un pays, deux systèmes et quatre nations
The European Discovery of Confucian Revolution: Anglo-American Philosophy and Social Science in the Shadow of Chinese Power and Moral Authority

# Better And Stronger Apart

HOW A NEW PARTITION OF THE BRITISH
ISLES CAN OVERCOME OUR BREXIT IMPASSE

One Country
Two Systems
Four Nations

*Dr David E Williams BA, DPhil (Oxon), FRSA*

ISBN-13: 9781019664263
**CIP?**

*For Stephen, an Englishman in Wales who voted to Remain,*
*and*
*For Charles, another Englishman in Wales, who voted to Leave –*

*– and to salute the genius of Stendhal (1783–1842), the French classic novelist and master of realism, who taught us all how to expose the character of our own country through the eyes of another people, thus allowing us to see ourselves, con brio, as others see us. If Stendhal put the French through the wringer for not being Italians, here the English Brexiteer will be given a bear hug of Celtic realism. This book, this trial of human reflection and will, is also a love letter to Greater Cardiff. So humour me; read on. But you have been warned.*

I am not here to argue with you;
I am here to help you pack your bags.

# Contents

# Acknowledgements

HERE I WOULD LIKE TO express my gratitude for the silent encouragement I gleaned, at moments of creative doubt, from the printed
page, in the form of thoughtful analyses of the causes and cures
of the issues raised by our Brexit dilemma penned by –

Alastair Campbell, editor of *The New European*
Nick Clegg of the Liberal Democratic Party
Isle Crawford, interior designer and author of *The Sensual Home*
Damian Flanagan, author and Chair of Didsbury Conservatives
    (Manchester)
Richard Florida, author of *The Rise of the Creative Class*
Carwyn Jones AM, the First Minister of Wales until 2018
Fintan O'Toole of *The Irish Times* (Dublin)
Richard North, political scientist, author and blogger
Matthew Parris of *The Times* (London)
Adam Price, Leader of *Plaid Cymru* (The Party of Wales)
Ivan Rogers (former UK ambassador to the EU)
Andy Street, Mayor of the West Midlands and former Managing
    Director of John Lewis

*Dr David E Williams BA, DPhil (Oxon), FRSA*

– and to extend a public word of thanks for timely bouts of political nagging and 'beratements', via phone, messenger and email, from Anthony Skirlick– unionist activist, California liberal to his fingertips, and comrade-in-arms since childhood.

# Preface: Beyond Brexit – the Celts, the English and a new partition

AFTER CENTURIES OF STRIFE WITHIN the walls of a single British state that insisted on governing all the peoples of these islands by oppressing too many of them, the Irish Free State was born in 1922. Twenty-seven years later it became the Republic of Ireland. This was the most important consequence of the first modern partition of these islands, and the most instructive constitutional lesson for all those who care about the future of their increasingly disparate and unhappy peoples.

Despite bloody resistance and bitter recriminations, the generation of 1922, Irish and British alike, decided that one state had to become two; the thing would not work any other way. Today, a century on, the imperative for another partition beckons. If – or when – the Leave and Remain nations decide to go their separate ways, it will be painful. Our first instinct will be to deny the need; our second will be to resist it. It is the point of this essay to think through these doubts and offer a defence of the right and freedom, in the spirit of America in 1776 as well as of Ireland in 1922, for the Leave and Remain nations to pursue their contrasting destinies; because half a loaf is infinitely superior to the half-baked Brexit currently on offer.

Having digested my argument for partition, many readers may still feel that the breakup of the United Kingdom is unthinkable and therefore impossible. This instinctive urge to cling together out of habit is powerful. The case for muddling through in traditional fashion is, however, an evasion of something profound and, I suspect, finally unavoidable. The Welsh realist would remind us that partition is a response to a divide that already exists, that existed long before the UK joined the European Economic Community in 1973, and that will endure even if we persist in our pretence that we are one country when in fact we are two: Leave and Remain.

The lessons of the American and Irish revolutions are clear. In 1776 and 1922, sentiment and inertia were overwhelmed by the necessity to live apart politically. The split between the Remain and Leave nations slices through the old unity of England and Wales. We are as divided as the Northern Irish have been, in a less vicious but finally more profound sense. Fiscally we cannot afford to go on as we are. Greater still than this practical challenge – the manifest inability of the UK as a state to govern, to pay and to defend its peoples – there is the open wound of mutual disaffection. Nations hold together out of a shared past and the promise of a shared future. This promise is doomed if we no longer want to share our country. The pro-Brexit campaign has put a sword through this desire.

*Dr David E Williams*
*Thomas Jefferson House, Bordeaux, France*
*4 July 2019*
*(Independence Day)*

# Introduction

## How to Read this Book

Our Brexit impasse is the consequence of our collective ignorance about two subjects of immense importance: the objective workings of the European Union and the scientific foundations of the free market. This ignorance has had a dire influence on how we vote, how the media reports the news and how our politicians shape policy. So the quickest and surest route to solving our Brexit impasse would be to bring our collective national intelligence to bear on the proper, unclouded understanding of the British and Irish place in the biggest, deepest and best-integrated free market in the world.

It is my suspicion, however, that our invincible ignorance of the EU and the Single Market will defeat my hopes for a quick and sure remedy to our Brexit impasse, and that therefore only an amicable divorce can save the day. This unhappy imperative feeds my strict criticism of the Brexit cause. I do not seek to convince the Brexiteer of the error of his or her ways. I suffer from no urges to score points or to vilify. Quite the contrary, I want only to demonstrate the necessity for us to live apart if we prove unable or unwilling to reason together.

*Dr David E Williams BA, DPhil (Oxon), FRSA*

## THE SPIRIT OF THE THING

Unusual in our age of dystopias, this essay is ripe with modern hope, with celebrations of English and Celtic creativity, of the splendours of our built environment and visual culture, and of the satisfactions and *élan vital* of business success. Nevertheless, at a perhaps more fundamental level, the spirit of the thing is animated by the kind of gentleness that writers such as Ernest Renan have classically associated with the Welsh. Our culture is quite simply too old to be brutal and unfeeling by default. Even when the Christian missionaries first arrived here, the Welsh had little heart to create martyrs.

Wales is another country. We intuitively sympathise with religious leaders, such as Pope Francis, who believe in social justice, in the struggle against poverty, and in the virtue of simplicity. Many poor Welshmen and women voted for Brexit, but in their poverty, we are still with them. Just as we stand with the resentful folk of Great Yarmouth, the battered of Barnsley and defiant of Dulverton. We just want more for them, and therefore for them to be more.

# CHAPTER 1

# Self-determination: the Remain nations at the door to freedom

*When in the course of human events it becomes necessary
for one people to dissolve the political bands which have
connected them with another and to assume among the
powers of the earth, the separate and equal station to which
the laws of Nature and Nature's God entitle them, a decent
respect to the opinions of mankind require that they should
declare the causes which impel them to the separation.*

— The American Declaration of Independence *(1776)*

WHEN THE AUTHORS OF THESE words decided to seek independence from English rule, their motives were varied; but America's founding fathers were united in their belief that government from London, however legitimate crown and parliament were deemed to be in the old country, posed an intolerable threat to American liberty, prosperity and identity. Being trampled over by Brexit England has sparked a parallel discovery among the English, Northern Irish, Scots and Welsh who voted to remain in the European Union. We find that our liberties, our communities, our prosperity and our identities have come under unacceptable pressure from what can only be described as 'Brexit tyranny'. Americans would not put up with this kind of misrule in 1776, and we will not put up with it today. As St Thomas Aquinas immortally observed, *Necessitas non habit legem* ('Necessity has no law').

In a democracy, there is an implicit but necessary limitation on majority rule. When a belligerent majority presses to the wall a confident, wealthy and organized minority (such as the Remain nations), any minority worth its salt (and we are) will eventually find a door. On our door is inscribed a single word: Freedom. In the wake of the referendum on UK membership of the European Union, Remain supporters believed, as many still do, that our sense of solidarity with the United Kingdom would survive this crisis of *our* confidence in the British state. Now, however, some of us who voted to stay with the EU are gradually reaching the conclusion that there is no longer an attractive and secure place for us within the United Kingdom as presently constituted. Is it time, therefore, for the Remain nations to dissolve the political bands that bind us to Brexit England and seek our own places, within the family of Europe, among the independent nations of the world?

Brexit tyranny has for ever banished the West Lothian Question about Scottish intrusiveness in English affairs; it was always bogus. The United Kingdom, a composite unity of four distinct nation-alities, cannot flourish as a political instrumentality to serve only English interests. It was the enormous swishing tail of English chauvinism alone that lashed the forces of Brexit discontent into open revolt; it is intemperate English nationalism alone that may prove to be the death of our United Kingdom. But on the central question there must be no illusions. If the Celts have no place of respect and honour, are accorded no deference to their constitu-tional position, here within these walls, we will find our door. For us now, since the Brexit vote, the would-be choice on offer is stark and unappetizing: a rampant Little England or a decaying United Kingdom. This is, of course, no real choice at all: either 'option' is a dead end.

The political reverberations of the Brexit vote have damaged the spirit of national solidarity between the Leave and Remain nations at its very heart. Too many wounding things have been said (most virulently on social media) that cannot now be unsaid. The epicentres of the resulting seismic turbulence are located not in Brussels, Berlin or Paris, but in Belfast, Cardiff and Edinburgh (the issue of the Remain nation of England centred on London will be addressed in Chapter 4 below). The Little England that forced Brexit upon us must therefore be put on notice that if Americans were not afraid to embrace national self-determination more than two centuries ago, the Remain nations should have no such fears today. Southern Ireland has since 1922 blazed this trail for us; but in any case, the urge to govern ourselves is no longer a matter of Celtic romantic sentiment but one of political, economic and social necessity.

Self-satisfied suburban contempt for Europe and angry rural nostalgia for a better yesterday among English voters forced the 2016 referendum upon us. Having few symbolic expressions of nationhood (even the St George flag is a ghost pennant of the medieval English state) and little real-world experience of specifically English governance, many English men and women have allowed themselves (again, mainly via social media in league with the tabloid press) to become prisoners of feelings so raw, so divisive and so unrealistic as to call into radical doubt the very foundations of our ever more brittle political system. The blind, uncontrollable rage of Little England in its desperation to be free of Europe has fed a calmer, more rational desire among the Remain nations to liberate ourselves from the irrational incoherence of Brexit tyranny. One thing drives the other.

The unity of a nation-state is a commitment that must be reaffirmed daily, and on 23 June 2016 the Brexit voter decided not to renew the marriage vows that have held our country together for centuries. This decision threatens us all with painful consequences.

Unless the *Daily Telegraph*, the *Daily Express* and their allies (including the cohorts of xenophobic keyboard warriors) call off the bulldogs, English Brexiteers may find themselves liberated from the European Union in ways that will radically undermine their place within the house of the United Kingdom of Great Britain and Northern Ireland. The time may now be approaching to sound the trumpets to greet the birth of the people's European Union; revolution from below, from the neighbourhood up.

The resulting paradox is clear: Brexit spells the end of the United Kingdom. Go stand on the pacified open border between Northern Ireland and the Republic, and observe the tide of commerce flowing by (can you hear the sound of Europe's anthem, Beethoven's Ninth?); brood on the shining, confident and exulting faces when a sea of Saltires laced with EU flags forms in Parliament Square in Edinburgh; thoughtfully and quietly appreciate the culturally diverse, polyglot and multinational European success story that is Cardiff, this dynamic heartland of a Welsh future that works – then tell me: what else could Brexit mean?

# CHAPTER 2

# Guardians of realism:
# the Welsh case for a constructive divorce

*A Welsh woman on the Titanic spots the iceberg and
alerts her cranky Little English travelling companion,
who retorts: 'Don't be so negative!' To which the Welsh
woman responds: 'I am not telling you how I feel
about it; I am just telling you that it is there.'*

## WHAT IS WALES FOR?

WHEN IN TUNE, THE WELSH are Europe's supreme masters of disinterested objectivity. This unrivalled gift for realism, something
that we share only with our Breton cousins in France, is a quite
splendid thing. It clarifies; it verges on the scientific. When you
describe a beautiful woman in England as beautiful, someone
will almost inevitably dismiss such praise as biased. Certainly the
Little Englishman is always on the hunt for suspect motives rather
than objective facts. In Wales, we have a practised eye for beautiful women, and when we see one, we will describe this beautiful
woman as beautiful simply because she is. In Wales, beauty is not
in the eye of the beholder but disinterestedness is. For us, beauty
is like perfect pitch; we conform to it, not the other way around.

The source of this talent for objectivity derives from a fruitful
and enabling absence: the Welsh don't care, in the first instance,
what the implications of reality are for our spiritual well-being

and our material interests. We are certainly indifferent to mere self-advertising or self-comforting pretensions, be they the inflated opinions of others or of ourselves. At the outset, all that matters is what is there standing in front of us. We are objective because we desire so little, while so many English men and women, like so many American men and women, are blinded from desiring too much, and therefore they have a great deal of trouble distinguishing what they want from what is possible.

Still, the axiomatic English assumption that 'Beauty is in the eye of the beholder' invites closer examination. In a general but decisive way, modern England is a culture of individualism, while Wales, traditional and modern, is a culture of unity. In this the English are often like the Americans and the ancient Romans (Think of the Latin tag *De gustibus non est disputandum*, 'There is no accounting for taste'), while the Welsh sympathize more with the French, the Italians and the classical Greeks. In a culture of individualism, the ultimate test of the quality of a novel or a painting is whether or not I like it. In a culture anchored in song, such as Wales, one is in tune or one is isn't. The standard is absolute, and it binds us. In a comparative way, one might observe that the last thing that would have occurred to an ancient Athenian is that the beauty of the Parthenon was a matter of opinion.

Now, how might this all matter to Brexit? Let us state the issue concisely as a set of propositions in which the British may or may not believe:

1. 'Beauty is in the eye of the beholder' (I suspect that both English Leavers and English Remainers may well subscribe to this influential aesthetic dictum).
2. 'Political reality is in the eye of the beholder' (only English Leavers appear to subscribe to this dangerous – indeed, in the case of Brexit, catastrophic – form of metaphysical solipsism.

3. 'Neither beauty nor political reality is, in the first instance, a matter of my subjective view alone' (this is the Welsh/ Breton metaphysical axiom, and this is the source of our disinterested objectivity).
4. 'Much, indeed, most, of political reality exists apart from and above any of my subjective preferences' (this is decisive: English and Welsh Remainers are united by their shared recognition of this axiomatic truth, acknowledging that the reality that stands apart from what I desire politically is composed of what Max Weber called 'inconvenient facts' that cannot be blinked away.

Here we find the metaphysical cause of Brexit and the invincible ignorance that makes our departure from the EU, the world's largest and best-regulated free market, what it manifestly is: a folly. The would-be democratic argument for Brexit as the 'will of the people' hits an immovable stumbling block if Brexit is a folly. Even if 99 out of 100 of the British electorate had voted for Brexit, this changes nothing if Brexit is indeed a folly. God could have voted for Brexit, and it would still be folly.

Now let us factor in the vulgar Brexit assumption that people who do not share the Leaver's preferences can be ignored because they are DPs –'different people' who do not quite qualify as members of 'our' tribe. As DPs, Remainers do not have to be listened to or engaged with intellectually because they are incomprehensibly disloyal: wilful traitors or the victims of corrupt judgement (the argument from motive, not fact).The temptation to spit on the Remainer in the street, to belittle him on social media or physically attack the Remainer MP with mortal intent may be traced back, in some obscure subterranean way, to the pernicious Anglo-American philosophical scepticism about 'other people's minds'. Whatever the sources and causes of Little English solipsism, of this rooted belief that there is no political or social reality aside from my private, ideological and nationalist preferences, the damage this self-inflicted obscurantism has wrought on our national life is manifest. Behold the strangest political beast of all: the patriot as metaphysical ostrich.

So the Welsh and the rest of the Celtic Fringe of the United Kingdom are owed a proper answer from the Brexit supporter, one is that true rather than just a self-flattering flight of aggressive rhetorical fiction. Did the English man or woman who voted for Brexit give any thought whatever to what this momentous decision would mean for the Celtic nations? What dangers it posed to the hard-won peace of Ireland? What pall it would cast over the vital Scottish campaign not only for social justice but also for prosperous self-mastery? What nightmarish dangers it might present to those obdurate Welsh communities north of the M4 who are so dependent on English largesse? Without a sober, convincing and contrite answer to this Celtic question, the United Kingdom is doomed – or should be.

Thus, in the gentle yet unflinching Welsh ability to see things as they are, we find the answer to the patronizing, ignorant and finally disloyal question that should never have been so breezily aired on British television: 'What is Wales for?' It is our national vocation as a considered responsibility to be the shepherds of realism. To see things as they are is the most precious thing we can do for ourselves and the other peoples with whom we share these islands. Being possessed of this gift means that from time to time we must tell hard truths to those who would evade such truths, to their peril and ours. This is what Wales is for.

In the context of the bitter and so far fruitless debate over Brexit, it is the Welsh gift for unclouded realism that leads us to commend the saving virtues of partition because half a loaf, as we shall see, is infinitely superior to no loaf at all, for the Leave and Remain Nations alike. There is a dimension of Welsh sentiment at work in this sober call for partition. The Welsh as a people have an enduring weakness for loyalty, for affection unto death. The powerful tale of love that is Tristan and Isolde is not German, not Scandinavian, but Celtic. At root, certainly for the Welsh, solidarity with those we care about is all we care about.

We have been ruled by the English for a very long time. Wales is England's oldest conquest. In contemplating a break with England (or part of it) after so many centuries, the prospect of a new national quest for Wales will inevitably evoke regret in many Welsh hearts over any break with our old masters. More revealingly, this parting of the ways will heighten our sense of concern for the fate of England. There is nothing ironic or craven about such feelings. So Free Wales seeks to bring to the Remain mentality not only the determination to save ourselves from the chaotic uncertainties unleashed in June 2016 but also to secure a home for our Brexit opponents, however dismissive and hostile Little England may be to the destiny of the four Remain Nations. Today we are all in need of salvation.


HALF A LOAF: THE GEOGRAPHY OF THE THING

Partition: how would it work in practice? I will address this question in easy stages over the course of this essay; here I begin with an overview of what this divorce will look like and how it will benefit all of us in these islands. Certainly the overarching goal of partition is to banish Brexit-inspired discord and confusion in favour of a more harmonious relationship between the Leave and Remain camps. We could thus put our present strife behind us.

Partition would mean replacing the British state in its current form with two successor states: the United Kingdom Federation (UKF) and the Kingdom of England (KE). The UKF would be the umbrella federation that unites and embeds what would become the four internally self-governing Remain nations (Northern Ireland, Scotland, Free Wales and Free England), and this in turn would serve as the basis for our continued membership of the EU. Brexit Wales might seek to belong to the Kingdom of England or, alternatively, take its place as part of the Kingdom of England and Wales (that is something for the Brexit camp to sort out for itself). Independence for Brexit Wales, as an ethnically cleansed republic or monarchy, is another option.

In this way, the meaning of Brexit will be transformed: Leave will mean leave; Remain will mean remain. With this very British compromise, the Leave camp will cease to be a threat to the dynamic multicultural prosperity and the humane values of liberal tolerance that the Remain nations share with most of the rest of Europe. Equally reassuring, the Remain camp will cease being an obstacle in the path of the Leave drive to break free of all things European. In this manner all shall have their prizes.


THE FOUR REMAIN NATIONS: SKETCHING THE MAP OF OUR FUTURE

Within the UKF, life should look and feel much as it did before June 2016: confident, prosperous, open to the world as part of the globe's largest economic market, and militarily secure under the double defence umbrella of NATO and the EU. Unlikely as it may appear, the fundamental Remain aspiration behind this plan for a new partition of the British Isles is 'no change'. We want to keep as many of our present political, economic and social arrangements exactly as they were on the day before the EU referendum. Logically, indeed, this must be the case if the UKF is to play its part in addressing the otherwise intractable dilemmas posed by revolutionary English nationalism. In the UKF, the monarchy, the pound and membership of the EU will remain unaltered, whereas in Brexit England the cry will be 'all change' to give that new state the maximum scope to reinvent itself in pursuit of the pure free-trading, anti-European and foreigner-free dream of England for the English.

One of the most soothing features of the Remain principle of 'no change' is the acceptance of the geographical results of the referendum – minus the Brexit tyranny. Such resolve to live inside the boundaries created by the referendum means that, within reason and with minimum strain, the partition of the old UK between the Remain and Leave nations will reflect the majority wishes in individual shires and cities. Granted, some adjustments may be necessary to reflect parliamentary constituencies and local government boundaries. Places as different as Cornwall, Birmingham, Swansea and Swindon may want to revisit their June 2016 decision. But the larger principle is clear: if your community, so defined, voted to leave the EU, you will leave, and if your community voted to remain, you will remain inside the EU. Thus, the comforting sense that one is in charge of one's own destiny would be affirmed across the redesigned and renewed fabric of the old United Kingdom.

## PARTITION: A COST–BENEFIT ANALYSIS

The headline issues that have dominated the politics of Brexit since the referendum can be approximated to a single messy, divisive and challenging conundrum. Brexiteers demand an end of the free movement of people ('taking back control'), along with liberty for the UK to negotiate new trade deals while retaining privileged access to the EU ('having your cake and eating it'). If Brussels will not surrender to this double Little English demand, there is the prospect of 'hard Brexit' ('going over a cliff').

Alternatives, such as continued membership of the single market or a customs union, would defend Remain nation prosperity and values at the expense of the Brexiteers' determination to see an incontrovertible end to both the free movement of people from within the EU and the judicial oversight of the European courts. For the Conservative and Labour parties, the core dilemma is the politically painful trade-off, most acute in but not confined to the northern English constituencies, between ethnic cleansing (getting rid of 'Johnny Foreigner') on the one hand and, on the other, overturning the economic foundations of the Remain nations in favour of a low-tax, privatized-NHS and tariff-free future ('glorious' or 'pie in the sky' depending on your perspective). Then there are technical issues to be addressed. Some of these challenges are politically explosive, such as the UK's financial divorce settlement with the EU, and others just exhausting (the monumental task of incorporating 45 years' worth of EU legislation into British law after Brexit).

A cost–benefit analysis of these issues within the broader scope of the many difficulties that Brexit presses on the British state will illustrate the true scale of the mountain that the Brexiteer insists we climb. At the same time, such an analysis highlights the virtues of partition as a sensible way towards smoothing paths into the future for both the Remain and the Leave nations. In fact, the majority of the problems that have piled up on the prime minister's desk in No. 10 Downing Street since the referendum vote can be eliminated at a stroke by keeping the Remain nations within the European Union. Below I present two lists: first, the set of tasks that the birth of a United Kingdom Federation will entail; and second, the benefits of partition for the new Kingdom of England. These two lists stress the gains from partition; the costs are obvious.

## Tasks for the new United Kingdom Federation (UKF)

1. The UKF would move immediately to revoke Article 50, thus securing the place of all four Remain nations within the European Union.
2. The UKF would affirm the security and openness of the Northern Irish border with Ireland and the EU, thereby

halting any attempt to replace the status quo with something impractical and dangerous.

3. The UKF would assume responsibility for Gibraltar, which would therefore remain within the EU, eliminating the potential for unnecessary border friction with Spain. The UK's remaining colonies and overseas dependencies would also be guaranteed in their security and prosperity as integral parts of the UKF.

4. The UKF as a member of the EU would assume responsibility for the legal status, pensions and well-being of the current million or so UK residents in other EU nations.

5. The UKF as a member of the EU would affirm the status quo with regard to the City of London, thus stabilizing and protecting our huge financial sector. The still larger sector of the UK's world-class service capability that is our highly profitable and highly exportable expertise in business support, legal, consultancy and auxiliary financial services is vastly in excess of domestic requirements. It requires access to foreign markets, and the UKF would assure it access to that of the EU, the deepest and least fettered market of all.

6. The UKF as a member of the EU would guarantee freedom of movement (the right to work and live) within the four Remain nations, thus securing the livelihoods and well-being of the roughly 3.4 million EU citizens from abroad who contribute so mightily to Remain nation prosperity. In so doing, it would help to redress the expensive and depressing consequences of a rapidly ageing society. In principle, the UKF would offer sanctuary for all the EU refugees, perhaps amounting to half a million people, who would face expulsion from the Kingdom of England. All the hard-working young people raising their families, paying their taxes and under-using the NHS would be made particularly welcome across the UKF.

7. Were the KE to refuse to meet any of the UK's current financial obligations to the EU, the UKF would strive to meet these in return for an adjustment in the amount of our future payments to the EU. This stance will mark the formal abandonment of the pursuit of British exceptionalism in Europe and the wider world.

8. All the supply chains that cross UKF territory would be secured. All foreign firms with manufacturing and distribution bases in the KE would be offered alternative homes within the UKF and, to the degree that it is within our powers, we would secure open transport links to and from KE facilities.

9. The pound sterling would be kept as the national currency for as long as the citizens of the UKF wished it to be so.

10. The UKF would remain a monarchy (the hint is in the name). The royal residences would continue as at present, with the single important exception of Sandringham in Norfolk, which would serve as the KE's premier royal home.

11. London would remain the capital of Free England and the UKF, and therefore all the institutions of the old United Kingdom would continue to be based there as long as the people of the UKF supported this.

12. All the EU institutions currently located in the UK would be asked to stay. To replace those already lost because of Brexit, the UKF would compete vigorously to provide a home for new institutions to deepen and reaffirm our institutional links with the EU.

13. The UKF would expedite negotiations with the KE on the management of the latter's closed borders with the UKF in order to make this transition as free from disruption as possible.

14. The UKF would assume responsibility for all the road, rail and air links through and between its territories in agreement with the KE in a manner consistent with the official border that will be established between the UKF and the KE. All ports (including tunnels, harbours and airports) in UKF territory would function as they do currently, while cooperative arrangements would be negotiated to ensure that ports in the KE (such as Dover) are open for *transit-only* commerce between the UKF and other EU countries in ways that will not undermine or threaten the closed character of KE borders. The 15,000 or so lorries that pass every day from the European continent into Kent would continue to roll through the otherwise closed Leave countryside to Greater London and beyond without hindrance or delay.

15. All universities, NHS hospitals and laboratories, farms, fisheries and factories in the UKF would continue to hire citizens freely from anywhere in the EU, to organize and participate in multinational EU research projects, and to grant admission for study and training here to all EU citizens as currently applies. The crisis that threatens social care, for example, in Scotland and elsewhere, because of a drastic decline in the number of workers from the rest of the EU would therefore be avoided.

16. Partition would instantly banish all Remainer worries about the production, transport, distribution and marketing of nuclear products, cars and car parts (consumer, commercial and F1 engineering), planes and plane parts (Airbus, Bombardier, etc.), health services and pharmaceuticals, technology, and consumer products more broadly, including our enormously important creative industries. Our vital service sector would thus be protected.

17. Behind the shield of EU borders, existing British manufacturing within the UKF would be preserved and enhanced. At the same time, the much larger economic flows of all kinds (including hardware/software bundling) that the deep preferential trading power of the single market uniquely provides will be exploited to the full across the UKF.

18. Finally, in the cause of future dynamism, the UKF would provide a secure legal and political home for the creative classes of England, Ireland, Scotland and Wales, together with all those people from Europe and across the globe who would share their gifts, talents and visions with us in the pursuit of prosperity and a decent life for all humanity. In this cause, the national motto of the UKF would be 'Tolerance, Talent, and Tempered Technology'.

## BENEFITS FOR THE KINGDOM OF ENGLAND (KE)

1. Brexit Britain reconstituted as the Kingdom of England would not be a member of the UKF, and therefore would no longer be a member of the EU. Indeed, the KE will never have been a member, and so it would not formally be leaving the EU. My working assumption is that the KE would refuse to meet any obligations, legal or financial, to the EU that might be deemed to attach to it as a successor state to the old UK government. The sharing of the national debt and the state pension system between KE and UKF would be subject to negotiation between these two entities exclusively.

2. The legal fusion of EU and UK law that has taken place during the past half-century would be swept away, leaving a *tabula rasa* or blank slate, with the KE free to adopt

whatever laws it wishes from the body of EU law and that of common law.

3. The KE would, in principle, have no foreign residents on its territory. My working assumption is that all EU citizens (including UKF citizens) would be denied the freedom to reside in, work in or visit the KE (I will revisit this question in Chapter 7). The nationalist Brexit goal of ensuring that 'England is for the English' where it most counts, that is, at the level of the neighbourhood, would therefore be achieved by fiat.

4. The KE would be free to create its own national bank and currency unburdened by the constraints and responsibilities of the Bank of England, the City and, indirectly, the European Central Bank.

5. The KE would, from day one of the partition, immediately be at liberty to pursue trade negotiations with any and all non-EU nations, including those of the Commonwealth. Brexit aspirations to 'British Empire 2.0' would thus be open to fulfilment. The only caveat would be that any form of social dumping that threatened the economy of the UKF and the European Union would be regarded as a hostile act.

6. The KE would be free to establish its capital anywhere within its territory. Milton Keynes or Birmingham might be among the candidates, as indeed might Barnsley, Barnstaple, Great Yarmouth and Middlesbrough, were priority to be attached to rubbing the noses of the governing elite in the values, opinions and prejudices of local communities in the provinces.

7. The KE would inherit no defence treaty obligations with any foreign power, and so would be free to negotiate any or none. Therefore the principle of 'splendid isolation' would be affirmed. All US military installations would be offered alternative homes inside the UKF or be regarded as islands of UKF territory within the KE.

8.  The KE would have no formal commercial, governmental, defence or transport ties with the European Union. Thus the hated link with Europe would be completely severed. A strict education in the realities of a WTO regime would follow.

9.  The Brexiteers of the KE would be free to abolish the despised French-invented metric system in favour of imperial measures, in the home, the shop, the factory, the laboratory, the armed forces and the science class. In like spirit, the 1971 decimalization of the national currency could be reversed in favour of halfpennies, sovereigns, guineas and the like.

10. All foreigners playing for English football clubs in the KE would be sent home, thus offering those who believe English sporting talent will thrive once the curse of foreign competition is banished from the pitches of Brexit England the chance to realize their dream. Only the issue of race and Englishness would remain to be addressed.

11. The productive creative classes of the cosmopolitan post-new economy – polyglot, multicultural and multinational, with their rooted commitment to the 'four Ts' celebrated above in the new UKF motto – would be expelled from the KE, or invited to flee or drain away of their own accord. Thus the KE would sound the fanfare for its longed-for and self-congratulatory retreat from the twenty-first century back into a romantic vision of a splendid past.

12. The birth of the KE would put paid to the often made threat that Brexiteers would greet (entirely possible) defeat in a second referendum on membership of the EU with violence and civil unrest. In place of strife, the soothing balm of partition is proposed. Nick Clegg's just call for a second referendum would thus serve as a legitimating transition to a final and conclusive vote to ratify partition.

# CHAPTER 3

# The M4 revolution: freedom's road from London to Cardiff

*Trees have roots; men have legs.*

— JEWISH PROVERB

MEN AND WOMEN ARE NOT trees; we leave the homes of our parents and shape new lives elsewhere. It is not rootedness but motion and the conquest of space that make us human. At least since the Irish Great Famine of the 1840s, the British Isles have been caught up in the age of mass migration. Millions of immigrants from these shores helped build the Empire and the United States of America. In circumstances favourable and unfavourable, for motives humane and inhumane, with results glorious and not so glorious, the British have long been a people in motion, and so they remain to this day. We come and we go, and sometimes we do not return. Home is where we make it.

The M4 motorway is a slab of concrete and asphalt that snakes its way from London, the capital of Remain England, to Cardiff, the capital of Remain Wales. This highway is more than just an impressive piece of infrastructure substantially completed in 1993; it is a novel, impromptu creation that embodies a state of mind. The importance of the M4 derives uniquely from the shared unity of purpose it gives to two of the four Remain nations that will form the United Kingdom Federation. Because it crosses the border between England and Wales, it embodies a dynamic, constantly moving channel of human ambition that binds globalized England to globalizing Wales. This makes the M4 a more precious bond today between the nations of these islands than even the English language – or rugby.

The M4 is a people mover. Up and down its length, the English and the Welsh, and everyone and anyone else who shares this region with us, migrate from one place to another, from one city to another, in search of personal, familial and community success and happiness. Observe how the M4 allows us to sidestep the defeatist language that would value 'somewhere people' over 'anywhere people'. The Remain nations at their most dynamic and prosperous are not populated by the mental heirs of feudal peasants tied to the soil. Like Galileo's planets, we move.

It is humanity so defined that transformed the M4, this almost sacred path of pilgrimage for the prosperous progressive (the M6 between Scotland and the north of England offers an instructive contrast), into an agent of the liberal revolution that gave birth to Remain Britain and Northern Ireland. Only the brilliance of the project of 'singularity in openness' that characterizes contemporary Scottishness, and the astonishing Irish reinvention of popular nationalism as a soft plural glue of multiple identities capable of holding a whole otherwise tormented island together can compare. So the M4 and its revolution merit the deep-breathing fixity of our most focused attention. Only in this way can we learn to appreciate why this business nexus is so important and what the M4, understood as at a motorway that became a region, reveals about this energy-channelling economic powerhouse that so firmly said 'No' to Brexit.

Let your eyes tell the story. Thus, one of the easiest ways of learning to appreciate the radical character of the M4 revolution is to visit one iconic place – Canary Wharf – and then travel to another – Cardiff Bay – and let the architecture of the thing allow you to take in the true scale of what has been accomplished in the four decades since the free-market innovations but also one-nation Tory reforms of the Heath–Thatcher/Heseltine–Major era transformed the UK after the English and the Celts once again came home to Europe.

## ARCHITECTURE AND OYSTERS

To many people, globalization is a bit of word magic, an abstraction, until an army of foreigners arrives in their villages, towns and cities, as it were, almost overnight. Serious words such as 'financial capital' and 'human capital' may seem like jargon from the lips of an MBA lecturer until you register the impact of these two kinds of capital on our built environment, the very architecture of our most dynamic cities and richest towns. The result of the conversion of capital and skill into architecture is anything but an abstraction. It is a productive hive of facts set in concrete, steel and glass that makes urban reality real to the eye and the hand, and so affirms the prosperity of Remain Britain that even the most bilious Brexiteer cannot deny or denigrate it.

The built environment is the key. When French explorers first stumbled on the stupendous ruins of Angkor Wat, they asked the Cambodian farmers who were working the paddies nearby how these imposing structures near Siam Reap came to be. 'They just grew here' was the self-serving deflection of an answer from a superseded people. There are sad, and saddening, places in contemporary Britain where the locals might similarly indulge in such deflationary wit about our cathedrals and universities, airports and distribution centres – but not in the Wales of the M4.

History does not depress the Remain voter; it inspires us. The architectural legacy of the Welsh capital's first economic revolution – under Lord Bute as commercial genius, the richest man in the world, the personification of King Coal – makes Cardiff's ambition for a more confident future just that much more plausible: we have done it once, and now we are doing it again. We are going to rival the splendours of our splendid past. How better to honour the achievements of our ancestors than to match them?

In this sense, Cardiff has more in common with the American frontier than with heritage Britain. The Welsh capital *as a city* is younger than San Diego, Los Angeles or San Francisco. Our great Victorian inheritance of imposing buildings that ooze confidence, from Lord Bute's neo-gothic Castle (our less grandiose but better-crafted answer to Citizen Kane's 'Xanadu'), the Hodge Building, the Howell Building and the rest of the imposing structures that populate St Mary's, down to the Pier Head House in the Bay, offer enduring reminders of the former greatness of our city. These stone and brick monuments silently fan self-belief today.

For an eye educated to see the world in this way, a certain vision of things takes hold. Therefore, when a denizen of Greater Cardiff travels to Newport or Swansea, and assumes a bird's-eye perspective over the centres of these cities of past achievement and future promise, the first thought of any confident citizen of the contemporary world (a subscriber to the *FT* or *Monocle*, for example) is that everywhere one looks opportunity lies in wait. Eagle-eyed from the outset, such men and women are primed and ready to learn fresh skills, launch a new business, start a family.

Always such dreams are grounded in reasoned confidence in our abilities to nurture a still finer future. Why? Because wherever we find ourselves along the spectrum of triumph and trial, victory and defeat, as we make our way through days of thick and thin, we are sustained by the conviction that our globalizing century is ours to master, now and collectively. If bad times knock us down, we get up, dust ourselves off, and return to the fight. The whole philosophy of the thing assumes a world composed of the choicest fruit of the recently resurrected glories of Swansea Bay: oysters (because for the cosmopolitan Remainer the world is our oyster).

## IN THE BEGINNING WAS THE M4

The first line of Goethe's *Faust* is a bold paraphrase of the opening of St John's Gospel: 'In the beginning was the deed.' The M4 as our deed took effective shape as a transport project haunted in its mature phase by a paradox; for it was the politician who waged war so pitilessly on the mining communities of the Welsh valleys who also laid the groundwork for the M4 revolution: Margaret Thatcher. And this paradox gives us another. In ways entirely unintended by Britain's first woman prime minister, with her worthy but old-fashioned notions of domestic thrift, the scrapping of the post-war system of economic controls, boards of trade and the like, unleashed the animal spirits of casino capitalism in ways undreamed of by many of the rather timid free-marketeers who drove the 'Big Bang' programme of the Tory government.

The effect was a miracle of unexpected consequences, but the economic advance that resulted from making London the financial centre of Europe has been astonishing. Canary Wharf is an architectural monument to this stupendous adventure in (leveraged) wealth generation and speculative bravado. In the shadow of this vast cash machine, the M4 has been transformed into a superhighway of capitalist borrowing, investment and stimulus. There are other such arteries thrusting their way in all directions from London, and they all provide the same unforgiving test of provincial vitality, vision and drive. Any region of the provinces with this kind of supercharged connection to Greater London that has not enriched itself since the 1980s is a failure, and therefore as an region it may, to an uncomfortable degree, have only itself to blame. On this subject, the culture of complaint that feeds the resentments of the Brexiteer cuts no ice whatever; economically speaking it is absurd.

Guided by the robust Remainer cast of mind, let us take a journey of the imagination along the formidable artery that transcends the divide (and wound) separating England from the Celtic Fringe, for it is the M4 alone, as we have noted, that connects the home counties with Wales in so economically miraculous a manner; only the great rail link from Paddington to Swansea compares in importance (slash the expense but bring on HS2; Cardiff is panting for this high-speed rail link). Think of the major urban centres served by the M4, from London's Hammersmith reaching north-west to where it brushes by Heathrow, then past Windsor and High Wycombe, and on to Reading (and, by natural economic extension, Newbury and Oxford), thence to Swindon, Bath and Bristol (the economic workhorse of the west of England) on the banks of the Severn and the great logistics centre that is Avonmouth.

From there we cross the border to Monmouth (the Welsh community with the highest per capita income), pass through the sprawling manufacturing centre at Filton Abbey ('Airbus land'), and then finally arrive at Greater Cardiff itself. Among all these English cities, only Swindon voted to leave the EU (which may explain why many gay residents find Swindon so boring they play in London). And therein lies the political warning for any Brexiteer who would make war on Britain's creative classes.

The Remain determination to succeed is but a hair's breadth, say the breadth of a well-earned fifty-pound note, from the Remain power and readiness to execute the anti-Brexit deed of deeds: the act of freedom that is national self-determination. At root, our call for partition cloaks a non-negotiable demand. Either the Brexiteer must compromise and concede the Remain nations their right to be free and prosperous (to our eyes, Leave Britain is neither) or we shall seek a divorce from Brexit tyranny. Either way, we are going to make freedom's bell ring.

GREATER CARDIFF: HE WHO PAYS THE PIPER

Of the four nations that comprise the United Kingdom of Great Britain and Northern Ireland, only one believes in the United Kingdom as a matter of settled conviction. That nation is Wales. And nowhere is the wisdom of this article of Celtic faith more prosperously on display than along the stretch of the M4 that runs through the south-east region of our nation. This region will provide Free Wales with its backbone. If and when the rest of our country, on its own or as part of the UKF, decides to overcome the traditional Welsh doubts about the price of 'getting on' in order to learn how to make our way in an ever more competitive world, the M4 corridor will serve as the hothouse and seedbed of our collective crusade for economic self-mastery.

Honouring the national character, we have breathed into life an efficient but almost stress-free form of Welsh capitalism: less impatient, more sharing; less elbows akimbo, more trusting; and better at balancing the competing claims of work and home. *Pace* Adam Smith, Daniel Defoe, Benjamin Franklin and other classical proponents of economic individualism, the pronoun that matters more to us in any definition of a Welsh kind of capitalism is not 'I' but 'We'. The M4 revolutionary is motivated by a collective quest inspired by an article of shared faith: my prosperity builds that of my neighbour, and vice versa.

And this brings us, once again, to the clarity of Welsh realism. From the vantage-point furnished by our national clear-sightedness, the true character of the economic conflict between the Remain and Leave nations is obvious: the Brexit bulldog is over-keen to bite the hand that feeds it. Thus too many Leave voters who feel 'left behind' want substantial handouts from Remain voters. And if this weren't enough, the Leaver seeks to lay waste to the very means that allow the Remainer to make the money that the Leaver so covets. In short, the Leaver wants the Remainer to row the boat of the British economy while the

Leaver drills holes in the bottom. The stance of the Leaver is, of course, muddled business thinking, but it does dramatize one indispensable truth: Remain Britain knows how to row.

The number of Remain voters may be slightly fewer than those of the Leave camp but we are, on average, younger, wealthier, more dynamic, more competitive, healthier, physically fitter and less obese, more open and more tolerant, more at ease with ourselves and others, more motivated and goal-minded, and therefore better trained and better educated. As a result of all these qualities we are more confident in our ability to make our way in the world because we can pay our way. And when and if we leave the old regime we shall take our tax base with us. This matters because as much as two-thirds of all Britain's productive power may reside within the borders of the Remain nations. Here you will find the dynamic armies of Britain's vital centre.

An impressive part of this productive power is located, as noted above, along the M4 corridor that stretches from London to Swansea. Via this modern Roman road made of concrete and will-power, a welcome wagon of talent, energy, ideas, investment and business opportunities makes its way daily from one of the greatest cities on earth to Remain Wales. In this Celtic here and this Welsh now, between Monmouth and the Gower, we have learned to exploit this dazzling cornucopia to create and sustain our own M4 revolution. After the fall of 'King Coal', the Welsh needed to learn how to row again, and we have.

THE EYE'S EMBRACE
Nowhere is the resulting reversal of Welsh fortune more formidably on display than along the waters of Cardiff Bay. In a sustained demonstration of provincial British grit and grip, the dereliction and despair of Cardiff's doomed docklands (inhabited by proud,

charming, ethnically diverse neighbourhoods of decent people who, through no fault of their own, were unable until today to produce enough, to consume enough and to save enough to sustain an economic renaissance) were seduced, over three decades, by a profit-making engine of growth that embodies the very essence of the post-coal resurrection of the Welsh nation. Spiritually, the most precious gift and most redeeming balm conferred on us by this communal act of urban rebirth is not money or buildings or services or tourist numbers (though all are enormously valued) but optimism and self-belief. In remaking the Bay we Cardiffians have, as it were, remade ourselves.

How did a specifically Welsh M4 revolution take shape? Where did this Celtic contribution to the vast Remain tax base, and this economy of confident abilities that has made it possible, come from? Part of the answer can be found in those two abstractions: the steady, gradual and well-paced growth of both kinds of capital, financial and human. This provided ammunition for our revolutionary advance. Quietly, just below the horizon of our collective social awareness, a vast pool of money, from London, the EU and beyond, has helped to sustain an impressive expansion of the skill base of the economy of south-east Wales.

This economic metamorphosis has reshaped our urban geography. And this revitalized sense of place brings us to a consideration of Cardiff Bay, one of the best-kept secrets of the UK's economic renaissance that has so enriched the pockets of the Remain nations and thereby made us respectable, well-off members of the family of Europe. The launch pad was provided by a massive infrastructural project: the Cardiff Barrage. Protecting the Welsh capital from the huge tidal flows of the Bristol Channel, the Barrage has transformed Cardiff Bay into a magnificent enclosed lagoon. Along this calm body of water fed by the Taff and the Ely rivers, Cardiff has erected a superb waterfront stage set and showcase for the new Wales.

Here is where Welsh modernity marries the iconic spirit of the Sydney Opera House with the synergistic 'spin-off' energies of places such as Boston's Kendal Square (home to MIT). Consistent with the new national ethos, Cardiff Bay is a quietly satisfying Celtic achievement because, most of all, it works. Thus, the Bay embodies all of the ingredients, human and architectural, of this M4 revolution that *we* have made. Turning our back on the Brexit poverty of resentment, Cardiff's motto is 'Investment, not handouts' (but if you give us a handout we will turn you a profit).

When this stream of investment first arrived from London after the dismal decades of post-coal decline, the money (and the faith) came from the British state; but it was soon followed by a tide of capital from the private sector. Together this alliance of public and private investment financed the transformation of the derelict docks and wharfs of the old coal depots into a gentrifying but still humane victory for contemporary urbanism: a low-crime, walkable and cycle-friendlier community (we are learning, still, from the Dutch and the Danes) of medium-density apartment blocks (so ensuring shorter commutes because less suburban sprawl), organized as a substantial governmental, pleasure, cultural and creative quarter; the best continental European analogy, in respect of both commuting times and civic function, may be modern Rome.

The collective realization of this *shared* vision of *shared* success has made Cardiff the urban anchor and unofficial heart of the nascent resort zone that is the Welsh Riviera (our weather tends to be much better than almost anywhere along the Bristol Channel), and so we proudly reign over Europe's youngest capital city. If the data gatherers at TripAdvisor are correct, Cardiff Bay has recently achieved the status of the fourth most attractive tourist destination in the UK. This Welsh secret is getting out; I blame the made-in-Cardiff TV series *Torchwood*.

So position yourself on the black slate steps of the National Assembly of Wales, with your back to this fine postmodernist building inspired by classical Japanese architecture, and take in the sweep of new buildings on your right that form an almost unbroken row of apartment complexes and yacht moorings, beginning out beneath St Augustine's in Penarth, and then marching, as if on parade, to the mouth of the Taff. This is Cardiff's re-imaging – an architect's semi-conscious dream – of Venice's Grand Canal in the practical language of the contemporary built environment.

Now look left. This brings into view our creative quarter, dominated by the BBC's television production studios. Then rotate on your heels to see the complex of shops, bars and restaurants that crowd the handsome promenade between the sea and two of the two supreme (but still restrained; this is Wales) architectural incarnations of Welsh modernity: the Richard Rogers Senedd Building, home to the National Assembly, and the Welsh Millennium Centre, the premier cultural venue and most visited tourist attraction in Wales, Cardiff's friendly act of grateful rivalry with the Basque capital of Bilbao. Here again the array of fine buildings, when approached from the water, evokes architectural memories of Venetian confidence and splendour.

The Bay is a monument to Cardiff's determination to succeed, and therefore not to be left behind. About this fact of our national experience, we must tolerate no Brexiteer fogginess. Nothing – not the money, or this architectural bonanza, or central government policy-making – has mattered more than the collective will of the citizens of Cardiff to reinvent themselves. To succeed one must desire success, and Greater Cardiff succeeds because we want it to. In this effort, Europe has been our ally, not our enemy.

## OUR CARDIFF: THIS COALITION OF THE WILLING

Who are the 'We' who have worked this urban miracle of willed collective advance? Their ranks include the urban planner armed with a gift for patient long-term thinking; the city father and mother who have made politics (more often than not) into the art of urban progress; the investor who believes in Cardiff's tomorrow and the creative mortgage broker who gives such investment focus and purpose; the veteran woman manager who keeps the St David's 2 Mall ticking over; the tough-minded businessman who harries builders and insurance companies until they give us quality construction; the hijab-scarfed chemist who looks after our health; the gay designer who reimagines the domestic setting of our lives; the Portuguese baker, Greek coffee merchant and Turkish-speaking Kurd and Cypriot grocers who transform our table; the English clothier who believes there is no ceiling on the Cardiff hunger for style; the Irish physical therapist who keeps our local MMA warriors fighting fit; the woman entrepreneur who reinvents the retail book trade in Cardiff Bay; the young aspirational working-class family man who makes sure he is home for the kid's evening bath after rowing the Taff with his mates; and the junior member of the Welsh National Opera chorus who sings her heart out when she helps bring the season to its close at Covent Garden. It is all enough to give ambition, talent and tolerance a good name.

All these people and more have made Cardiff Bay one of the efficient dynamos that have contributed so magnificently to the capital's rebirth. The Bay is another pair of sturdy shoulders in this great Welsh scrum of urban enterprise that unites all of the city's pivots of growth, ranged alongside the St David's shopping malls and our Parisian-style arcades (Cardiff's retail heart is one of Britain's most popular consumer destinations because it is one of the most convenient and best organized), in fruitful alliance with the all-weather Millennium Stadium (Europe's largest roofed arena and Wembley football's home away from London); the new palaces of steel and glass that crowd the Cardiff Central Railway Station; the Newport Road of large retail outlets (our salute to Southern California); and then outwards to the north and east the industrial zone that stretches from Shirley Bassey's community of Tiger Bay to the M4, and finally to the west, where one passes through the prosperous farms and confident suburbs set in the rural splendours of the Vale of Glamorgan that surround our growing national airport. That airport gives us our indispensable link to Europe and the world beyond, a continent and a world we do not fear.

In this capital of capitalism with a human pace, Cardiffians do not know how to spell 'left behind' because we would never allow it to happen to us. We are committed to making our city a better place to live, work and study for everyone who has chosen to make a home here, regardless of where they come from and how long they want to stay with us. This collective determination is the most important quality that distinguishes what is best in the Remain nations from what is most defeatist about the Leave camp. The unofficial symbol of anti-Brexit Cardiff is a dragon with a pair of bootstraps.

### WHITE VAN REVOLUTIONARIES AND THE GOOD LIFE

The contemporary rise of Cardiff is the embodiment of the Welsh contribution to the vital centre of the life of our nation (the life of the United Kingdom that the Brexiteer, English and Welsh, is so keen to diminish). The animating spirit of Cardiff Bay represents a human triumph over traditional Welsh pessimism. When I first arrived in the Welsh capital to work nearly twenty years ago, every fine day was greeted with the dismissive cry: 'Ah, but it won't be nice tomorrow.' Thanks (warily) to global warming and the micro-climate that extends from the Bay to Cowbridge and Barry (almost), this meteorological nay-saying carries less conviction.

Today one complains about the weather in Cardiff Bay more out of habit than on the evidence of the senses. The subjective impression of warmer temperatures, less rainfall and brighter days reflects a broader optimism about the city's enhanced material prospects and the sheer pleasure of living in a young and dynamic community where so many people appear to be making a good fist of life while still having the time to stop and chat with friends and strangers. This civilized balance between productivity and leisure ensures that each new morning arrives with the promise of chance human encounters to affirm our sense of communal solidarity with each other in the making of our collective prosperity. Does anywhere else in the United Kingdom come close to this near perfection? Being Welsh, we hope so, because our first impulse is always to share.

This 'smart city' with a human touch is our mecca of civic optimism. The occasional media portrayal of the remaking of the Bay as an unequal pantomime struggle between greedy property developers and urban innocents who just want to wander around Mermaid Quay at the weekend wilfully misses the point. Thousands of hands have contributed to the regeneration of the old Cardiff dockland, and hundreds of small and medium-sized businesses now make a respectable living from serving the needs of the families and businesspeople who live in the thousands of apartments that have been built along the Cardiff Barrage. The ugly mud flats of low tide have been banished for ever, while a fine bird sanctuary as well as the now pollution-free Taff and Ely rivers provide healthy homes for a variety of wildlife (here we shall not speak of the seagulls).

In this way Cardiff Bay provides employment for hundreds of repairmen, window cleaners, and delivery staff who bring groceries, medicines and the post to our doors. There are carpets to be cleaned, apartments to be dusted, boilers to be maintained, walls to be painted and repainted, flooring to be put down, tiling to be sold, selected and laid, heating systems to be installed and serviced, furniture and appliances to be displayed and delivered, curtains to be measured and hung, televisions and computer systems connected and maintained, and public green spaces to be planted, mowed, trimmed and kept tidy. In this way we have found and secured employment for an army of small enterprises, many of them managed by youngish people who have found homes in or near the Bay.

And this brings us to the Cardiff attitude to money. You invite someone into your apartment in the Bay to provide this business product or service. A price has been agreed from the outset. When the job is well done, the price set is paid at once and in full. There is no haggling or evasion about paying what is due. We assume that a reasonable price is what has been offered, and we price our own services with similar reasonableness. Small businesses thrive in this city that is wealthy enough to give confidence to the entrepreneur that he or she can turn a profit here every day, on the day. If you seek evidence for the attractions of this self-lubricating form of capitalism, just ask any ambitious Swansea man or woman who does business in the capital.

Brexit would undermine this business culture of trust, efficiency and sustained profit. My partner and I buy apartments in Cardiff Bay, decorate and improve them, and put them back on the market. Despite the pall of Brexit, we are still in business and still making a profit, but the Brexiteer's war on British commerce has not helped. We source furniture, wallpaper and kitchen units from abroad. The sharp fall of the pound in the immediate wake of the referendum vote significantly increased our operating costs. The subsequent fluctuations in the value of sterling against other currencies, notably the euro, the US dollar and the yen (to cite those most relevant to our business) have made calculating costs trickier.

Furthermore, the advantage of Cardiff property becoming cheaper (because of sterling's decline), and therefore more of a bargain to potential foreign buyers, has been eroded by the xenophobic war cries of the Brexiteer. Quite reasonably, foreign investors in Cardiff Bay want to be reassured that they will not be hassled at passport control at Heathrow. Indian mothers whose children might want to study for an MBA at Cardiff University want to be confident that their daughters and sons will be safe from official discrimination by the Home Office, afforded decent treatment by the police, landlords and local government, and as well insulated as possible from informal abuse inflicted by the odd Brexiteer racist on the streets of the Welsh capital.

If our business drops off because of Brexit anti-business posturing, our need to employ painters, tilers, electricians, plumbers, furniture wholesalers and delivery people of all kinds declines. And such declines, as they ripple across the economy, adversely affect the plans and ambitions of white van man and woman as they seek to build their futures and those of their young families. Most revealing of all, television interviews, newspaper articles and social media interventions all suggest that the Tory governments that have held office since June 2016, along with the UKIP supporters and the stereotypical Labour-voting Brexiteers, *do not care* about the damage they are inflicting on the British economy. Certainly no pro-business government would have ever intentionally imposed this intolerable deadweight of uncertainty – an uncertainty that is entirely the consequence of the political vanity and self-destructive, romanticized, nationalist sentiment of the Brexiteer.

## Not *Les Misérables*

The naysayer, the chauvinist and the handout-taker find no natural home in Cardiff Bay – but babies and children do. In contrast to the rapidly ageing character of Brexit Wales, Free Wales is the home of baby boomers who have become well-exploited grandparents. So, for example, anecdotal evidence suggests that Cardiff Bay, in ways that belie its image as an adult pleasure zone, is an incubator for young families who thrive on our mastery of the life–work balance. The indispensable luxury of time for a proper home life ensures that this city stays youthful, vital and married. And this explains one of the most striking features of modern Welsh urbanism: everywhere here one encounters babies and young children – in whom we take as much pride and pleasure as any Latin village or town on the Mediterranean. And this gives Cardiff Bay its own unpretentious meme: a child's tricycle parked at the doors of our opera house.

In this way, Cardiff Bay's army of prosperous young couples with babies confounds the dispiriting trend towards poorer and older societies with declining populations one finds elsewhere. This youthful revolution is possible because medium-density housing, properly maintained and enjoyed, ensures decent homes for perhaps a quarter of the city's young population within the confines of Cardiff Bay alone, and this very concentration of residential space reduces commutating times. One can in fact make a quite respectable income both working and living south of Callaghan Square.

In an inner city of trim and sprightly walkers, we use our cars sparingly. Furthermore, for longer journeys, our army of taxi drivers provides a cheap alternative to the considerable costs of car ownership. Our taxi drivers are ethnically diverse and sufficiently numerous to provide hundreds of jobs for the recently arrived, the newly unemployed, and men (and some women) who must look after ageing parents. And how is this taxi trade sustained? By servicing our huge influx of students, many from overseas, the thousands of concert goers and sports fans from England, and tourists from everywhere. (Tell me truthfully, are there any communities in the south of England where nobody has been to Cardiff's Arena and the Millennium Stadium?) When Newport hosted the Ryder Cup and Cardiff the NATO and G7 summits, even the local prostitutes apparently mobilized our taxi army.

This brings us to the tetchy subject of Brexit anti-elitism. The majority of the army of business people, young and old, who serve the Bay and secure the quality of our life here are not university-educated, although Cardiff can boast four universities. Training colleges are often the key. An impressive number of our young people, some in the early twenties, spend just enough time learning a skill and then working for experts in their trade of choice to master this trade in order to launch their own businesses or enter into partnership with their former employers. Thus the sole trader becomes a limited company.

In the same spirit, the built environment that Cardiff Bay inherited from the Age of Coal provides low-rent warrens where those of talent but little capital can start a language school or a photography business, launch a small research unit, open a talent agency or a liaison office for lobbying politicians and the civil service. Most revealingly, these old banks and insurance offices provide homes to the legal eagles, programmers and number crunchers for back-office financial services for London firms – and this brings the M4 miracle full circle.

Cardiff Bay mocks the divisive and unhealthy Brexit language that sets the successful against the poor, the educated against the uneducated. In this part of Remain Wales, impressive numbers of our young couples find the kind of jobs that allow them to afford decent housing, either to rent or to own, or first one and then the other. This quotidian success of the property market goes a long way towards ensuring that both partners as future parents get a decent material start in life, all in a setting of successful modernity where the very air tastes of sea salt and optimism. Unless these young people are refugees from the Welsh valleys, few of them know anyone in the Bay who has been left behind. As Cardiffians, all of us are pursuing our own vision and version of multicultural globalization, with its many dangers, temptations and challenges – but mainly opportunities. Our vim and vigour come with a chaser of realism; but, most of all, we are undefeated.

# CHAPTER 4

# Free England: the greatest remain nation and the undefeated champion of globalization

*Since the Referendum of 2016 the old divisions of English and Celtic life—class, region, education, tax bracket and sectarianism (in Northern Ireland)—have been overshadowed, perhaps irreversibly, by the Leave vs Remain tribalism. This realignment has placed extraordinary pressures on the British constitution, on the unity of our political parties, and on the concept of 'Britishness' as a kind of soft cloth to restrain and quiet our nationalist urges. On the subject of diversity and divisiveness, the UK has much to learn from the Irish Republic. But the most striking and unexpected revelation has been discovery that voter preferences about immigration and free trade align almost too perfectly with how we view blood sports, the death penalty, gay marriage, feminism, Islam, professional expertise, ethnic racism and eating olives. Is to disagree about Europe to disagree about everything?*

## The vital centre

Free England; Free Wales: what's in a name? Remain voters are free because we are liberals in two senses: we support freedom (respect, tolerance, civil rights, equality and justice for ourselves and others) and we support the free market (including the free movement of goods, services, money and people). We believe in Voltaire and Adam Smith, and this gives intellectual coherence to our commitment to the values of the European Enlightenment and the virtues of strictly regulated, well-taxed capitalism. These two principles govern the life of the European Union. We are therefore free in ways that the Leave nations are not. Indeed, we are the embodiment of freedom in the modern world.

This 'we' forms the *vital centre* of our national life. Indeed, this vital centre is the human heart of liberal civilization around the globe. Thus, the lively diversity that feeds the prosperity of Greater Cardiff also drives the globalizing economies of London, Glasgow and Dublin. In this sense we are at one with the forces of progressive wealth creation on the march everywhere across the liberal world, from New York to Paris, from Sydney to Vancouver, from Berlin to San Francisco. Socially, we work hard (and probably play too hard), but mainly we revel in the pleasures of our families and shared communities. Intellectually, we are eco-friendly and techno-friendly: we read *The Economist* (or know someone who does). Politically, we are crusaders for inclusive globalization and universal tolerance. We practise what we preach. We are the future's brightest face.

We of the vital centre are vital in both senses: spirited and indispensable. This vitality unites the Celtic Fringe with Free England. Demographically, we matter. Indeed, the free men and women who made the M4 revolution revolutionary, together with the communities across the Remain nations who share our values, represent the industrious heart of the British polity. As the indispensable core and pivot of the UK economy and electorate, we are the people who make Britain work, who borrow to invest so we can better make our way in the world, who generate, without tax evasion or secret wealth accounts in Panama, the bulk of the nation's tax revenues and national insurance contributions, who run and serve the majority of its businesses, large and small, and who therefore ensured that so much of the United Kingdom was, until June 2016, a place worth living in. This vital centre provides the tough. grounded infantry of any successful Remain resistance to reactionary Brexit tyranny. We could win a second referendum, and having won this battle, we could then lead our nation to a peaceful partition.

In the language of British sociology, the vital centre is the aspirational working class made good. These folk are what Max Weber would have termed our 'ideal type'. Called to freedom, it is this rather agreeable and attractive regiment of tolerant and hard-grafting Celtic and English men and women, at once ordinary and confident, who have made the M4 revolution; not the despised metropolitan elite of Brexit mythology. In our millions, we are the uncommon heroes of the twenty-first century. As members of the urban creative classes, we are making a future for the world with our spiritual comrades-in-arms, whom you will find wherever dynamic vitality has been unleashed, from Bangalore to Shanghai, from Singapore to São Paulo, from Muscat to Lagos.

We revel in our well-earned place among the ranks of the vital centre of humanity. Our quiet optimism, grit and grip contrast sharply with the mental outlook of the Leave nations. First and foremost, we are not xenophobes. We are committed to cultivating a hate-free democracy, while the Brexiteers have made Europe the scapegoat for all their destructive and unwarranted fears, just as the Nazis made the Jews the chief scapegoats for all of Germany's woes after the First World War. Different target; same rhetorical method.

The Brexiteer is not a Nazi; but he is too easily tempted by the siren call of ethnic cleansing, of the dream of England for the English (there is an unhappy Welsh analogy). Hitler gleefully seized on the nasty expression 'stab in the back' when castigating the human pillars of liberal Germany's Weimar Republic: social democrats, Catholics, cosmopolitans, homosexuals, liberals, labour union organizers, brave Protestant pastors, communists but mainly Jews. Does a day now pass when the accusation of 'stab in the back' is not hurled at the Remain cause by enraged Brexiteers on social media in Britain? Granted, there is a vast distance between the horrors of the Third Reich and the dangerous fulminations of Nigel Farage and Jacob Rees-Mogg, but the distance can be narrowed. Is this not the lesson of the 'Windrush' scandal? What else is one to make of Theresa May's apparent determination to inflict the fierce judicial rigours of the so-called 'hostile environment' on migrants to this country, people whose only crime is that they are not English by birth?

The enlightened Remainer will have none of this. The technological war of the Brexiteer on our electoral democracy is unacceptable. We say 'no' to the black arts of data dumping, no to unforgivable alliances with foreign 'dark web' boiler rooms, no to billionaire conspiracies *à la* Trump-land, and no to the scapegoating of Jews (then and now), Muslims, Poles, Romanians or anyone else the Leaver would first vilify and then persecute. On this subject, we are all spiritual heirs of France's pro-Semitic response to the late-nineteenth-century Dreyfus scandal, heirs of Emile Zola's immortal *J'accuse!*.

Some wit has recently observed that the supporters of Brexit represent an unholy alliance between the greedy and the desperate: *Pirates of Penzance* capitalism meets premature death by crisp bag. This bludgeoning stereotype exaggerates the point, but not by as much as one would like. Among the ranks of our vital centre – English, Irish, Scottish and Welsh – one finds neither our equivalent of America's broken, opiate-plagued underclass nor that of its tax-shy billionaire 'one-percenters'. Within the Remain nations, our lives are less burdened by the resentful xenophobes who refuse to treat the foreigners in our midst with respect and decency, and we feel less threatened by the demoralized working and lower middle classes who believe that Britain owes them a living.

These unhappy people form the smouldering, abusive ranks of Brexit's army of discontent. By voting to leave the European Union in the 2016 referendum, they made it clear that they want no place of honour and distinction among the dynamic, prosperous, liberal-minded free-marketeers and pro-Europeans who constitute our vital centre. The Labour and Conservative parties must today choose which of these peoples, Remain or Leave, they are going to serve.

Across the United Kingdom, the vital centre is no prisoner of the past. Confident of our future, we get on with the present. You will find these hopeful and proud citizens of the twenty-first century clamouring on to the packed morning tube trains in London, dreaming up another video-game platform in Dundee, crowding into lecture halls at a training college in Reading or Manchester, doing a finance deal in front of some splendid Victorian façade in Glasgow, building a part or devising a system for Bombardier outside Belfast, testing smartphone wafer technology in Cardiff, or writing another global bestseller in a quiet home in Scotland. This vital centre, the liberal core of four free Remain nations, deserves a state of its own presided over by a government that shares its commitment to liberal values and capitalist prosperity for all. This commitment is the one thing that Brexit Britain cannot and will not give us.

And so we arrive at the question of England. The vital centre of English life is quite simply indispensable to the Celtic Remain nations as we approach our hour of self-determination and therefore peaceful liberation from Brexit tyranny. The decent and dynamic men and women of liberal England will determine the shape of our national future by forcing the United Kingdom to choose between two contrasting visions, two philosophies of life, and two ways of being in the world today that brook no compromise. We need an answer to a question worthy of Kierkegaard: either/or. Which will it be? Which England?

THOMAS HOBBES AND THE TRIPLE CRISIS OF
THE BRITISH STATE

Wales is divided in its soul. It is two countries pretending to be one. And so is England. The chasm revealed by the Brexit vote of raw disaffection, unshared values, conflicting identities and clashing national outlooks cut most bitterly among the English. The campaign to leave the European Union has bludgeoned us into the unhappy realization that the Remain nation of Free England is joined at the hip to an angry and bullying, benighted and delusional Brexit Siamese twin. This Leave twin is burdened with an unenlightened and uncivilized world-view that makes him all but impossible to live with. The division of the soul revealed by the vote is putting unacceptable pressure on our collective ability to govern the United Kingdom effectively and therefore to keep our country whole. Behold the spectre of the partition of England.

In this time of the breaking of nations, Brexit is devaluing the Westminster model of government by exposing its fundamental flaws. In short, this model of parliamentary success is incapable of coping with the new excesses of English nationalism. Our two major *English* political parties are floundering because they are both attempting to reconcile two irreconcilable philosophies of government, capitalism and national identity: liberal tolerance and the well-regulated marketplace on the one hand and, on the other – forgive the caricature – a Little English blend of batty authoritarian xenophobia and robber baron capitalism. The result is a British re-enactment of the destruction of the Whig Party in the United States when it attempted to do the impossible before the American Civil War: to reconcile feudalistic Southern slavery with Northern emancipation and a continental-scale free market for labour. The intellectual and practical challenge for Scottish Tories is obvious and will be considered at length in Chapter 6 below on independence for Scotland.

This ideological circle cannot be squared; it is a matter of principle. Neither Labour nor the Tories can simultaneously serve two masters. The interests and values of the Leave and Remain camps are that radically in conflict. Electorally, the Remain camp may now be able to defeat the Leave camp; but such a victory would be conclusive only if it produced a change of heart. Hence the question: do first-past-the-post election results ever alter anyone's most deeply held beliefs? Another referendum can overturn the results of the first, and help us move forward. This would be a victory for realism and rationality; it would skewer the argument that democracy legitimizes Brexit chaos; but referendums may magnify our divisions before they heal them.

In themselves, referendums cannot make us whole. The defeated side will just lie in wait for another chance to win. Think of Trump's America. The Confederacy that was crushed in the Civil War over a century and half ago now has a president of its own in the White House. In Britain, as in America, the ballot box is not designed to alter hearts and minds; it assumes hearts and minds look after themselves. This is why the Westminster model cannot save us from ourselves – but partition can. We need to hold a second referendum to overturn and thereby delegitimate the first, and then to proceed to create our two successor states; because a new Kingdom of England alone will meet the desperate and uncontrollable urge of the Brexiteers to be masters of their own house, however reduced it may be.

On this subject, the iron logic of partition is all but irresistible. At root, we British no longer agree about what the state is for or what unites us as a people. The Tory descent into policy incoherence; the long evasion of cabinet debate over the most serious diplomatic and public policy challenge facing this nation since the Second World War; the repeated indulgence in gross self-deception by Theresa May and her ministers; and the collective failure of Britain's political culture (the BBC included) to understand and explain to the electorate the complex nature of our ties to the EU and why we profit, on so many levels, from belonging to Europe: all this has come close to shattering the national faith of many Remainers who have previously held an unshakeable belief in the 'Mother of Parliaments'. To state the point once more for emphasis, our future path must be made clear and exact: one more referendum to strip away the fake patina of legitimacy of the 2016 vote, and then a vote for partition to make a fresh start for everyone in these islands.

In 1921, a single state governed the totality of these islands: the United Kingdom of Great Britain and Ireland. In 1922, this single state became two: the Irish Free State and the United Kingdom of Great Britain and Northern Ireland. Today, we need another state to cope with our desperate and disordered politics: the United Kingdom Federation. This will offer our vital centre a political home to stand alongside the Republic of Ireland and the new Kingdom of England.

Only a new partition offers a rational and enduring cure for the triple crisis now threatening the British state. In weighing this claim, it may be of use to draw on the philosopher's unique command of the only full-blooded ideas that count here. Think of Thomas Hobbes (1588–1679), the greatest European political thinker that England has produced. His ideas were decisively shaped by the English Civil War, the last violent breaking point in our national life before the Irish Question. Brilliant and incisive, Hobbes would today judge the whole sad business of Brexit with unsparing harshness.

Our problems come in threes. First there is the severity of the recent cutbacks to Britain's military capabilities (the improvident budgetary axe has ensured that our new £3.1 billion aircraft carrier cannot be protected by the Royal Navy without French frigates). Then there is the intractable struggle to impose austerity and live with the social consequences. Finally, there is the Brexit-provoked crisis in the capacity to govern Great Britain and Northern Ireland as a unity. Confronted with this triple failure of government, Thomas Hobbes would have judged these humiliations to be a fatal blight on the United Kingdom's claims to be a credible sovereign power.

What Hobbes famously called the 'social contract' between ruler and ruled has been broken: the Britain that voted for Brexit cannot govern the country, cannot pay for the country and cannot defend the country. A state that cannot do these things is not a state. And a state that is not a state can neither exercise sovereignty nor 'take back control'. By virtue of this irresistible Hobbesian 'cannot', the chief constitutional ambition of the Brexiteer – authentic national sovereignty – is reduced to what it has always been since the 1956 humiliation of Suez: a dead thing but our own.

## THE STRANGE DEATH OF TUDOR ENGLAND

So let us consider the matter of England once again. If and when partition comes, Free England will be the pivotal friend and ally of the other Remain nations; the true hero of this crisis of our national disunification and redefinition. The success of a dynamic Free Wales, a Scottish nation that governs itself within the securing walls of the United Kingdom Federation, and a Northern Ireland constitutionally separate from the Republic but commercially and spiritually united with it inside the European Union: all this depends crucially on the support, the strength and the wealth of Free England, the hub of our vital centre.

This reliance of the liberal, free-trading and pro-European Celtic nations on this Anglo-Saxon economic dynamo highlights the catalytic contribution of the Brexiteer's campaign, five centuries after Henry VIII, to the rebirth of the English man and woman who is proud to call him- or herself 'a European'. No unintended consequence of Brexit may prove to be more important to the successful nurturing of our separate national destinies than the rebirth of this most ancient form of the overarching civilized identity that we Europeans, certainly in the Latin Catholic West, all shared before the Reformation. Thus we may be witnessing the strange, interminably delayed death of Tudor England – and not a moment too soon. One has only to pause in one of the more splendid of the quads of Oxford's Christ Church to imagine the resurrection of Cardinal Wolsey's vision of England playing a full, enthusiastic and loyal part in the life of Europe.

Today, since the US presidential election of 2016, Europe has become a unique fortress of liberal values and regulated economic dynamism. On the front of the culture war, homosexuality offers one of the supreme litmus tests for liberal tolerance in the contemporary world, and the EU, certainly western Europe, offers as secure and agreeable a place for the gay man or woman to live a life of dignified acceptance as anywhere on earth. This web of legal rights and humane values must be protected. While the United States fights out its own culture war, the EU must assume more of the burdens of the liberal superpower that the contemporary defence of liberal civilization demands.

The debate over the dangers of a European superstate has tended to focus exclusively on the threat strong centralized institutions may pose to local interests and liberties. This argument neglects the larger challenges posed by other superpowers – Russian assertiveness, American unpredictability and China's new global reach – to European life. On more than one front, Brussels is already rising to address this challenge. Is there any institution of government outside China today that has the power, the will and the effectiveness to take on Amazon over tax and the Trump administration over trade other than the European Commission? It is Brussels that is keeping chlorinated chicken and pork sprayed with lactic acid off our tables. On these battle fronts, the European Union is our sword and shield (the European version of the sharp-edged *Caladbolg* of Welsh mythology).

In like fashion, a pan-European army modelled on the grand coalition that defeated Napoleon would make Moscow more cautious and tragedies like Syria's less likely: 1815 and all that. In the defence of this magnificent continental-scale cause, Free England and the rest of the United Kingdom Federation would stand and fight with our European friends and allies for European liberty. And the UKF could make a difference because we know how to stand and fight. We must just learn, once again, how to pay for it all.

The millennial promise of the kind of security, order and prosperity that Imperial Rome guaranteed before the chaos of the barbarian invasions calls out to us today. The strength of Europe and the promise of the still greater strength of our Europe as the new Rome carry symbolic weight. The Statue of Liberty was France's gift to the United States to commemorate the centenary of its birth. If the forces of illiberal reaction finally triumph, God forbid, over 'the city on a hill' that has been America since 1776, then we will ask for this stone embodiment of 'The Lady with the Lamp of Liberty' to be returned to the Old World homeland that conceived her. We shall have her back and make her safe. In this way the old ways will become the new, and the Old World will transcend the New. How is that for a declaration of independence?

The symbolic importance of the Statue of Liberty should alert us to yet another potential danger. The current bitter paralysis of American government has encouraged the script writers of televised political thrillers – *Homeland* and the like – to imagine the previously unimaginable: the descent of the United States into a form of quasi-authoritarian demagoguery that might push this democracy to the brink of regional or national civil disorder. As yet, these imagined dangers remain imaginary. Furthermore, the US is a robust society with a robust political system, so I continue to be optimistic about its power to transcend and therefore survive one of the most divisive hours in the American experience since the Civil War of 1861–5 that left the South in ruins and as many as 750,000 dead.

Just the same, a timely exercise in risk assessment might be wise. Certainly, the bare ghost of a shadow of another 'War Between the States' might unleash a potential flood of political refugees back across the Atlantic, this time from the New World to Europe. Fear alone might create a human tide vastly larger than anything Syria has inflicted on us. We would have collectively to decide whether to support Canada in its supreme hour of crisis by opening our borders to these grandchildren and great-grandchildren of those who left these shores for America a century or more ago. The pull on the heart would be enormous. And having decided to do the right thing and receive the masses and elites of America's teeming shores clamouring for refuge, we would have to organize on a continental scale. Enter the European Union.

All these practical considerations should shape the debate today over what European-ness means in the twenty-first century, to our white majority and to our ethnic minority communities, be they Asian, Middle Eastern, African, West Indian or Latin American. Furthermore, any democrat, of whatever colour, creed or ethnicity, who calls the European Union 'home' should brood hard on the discussion in Chapter 7 below of the dangers posed to Europe and European cohesion by the very idea of the ethnic cleansing of Brexit England and Wales. Before we turn to that testing issue, that trial of blood, we must be prescient about the geographic shape of Free England as the country upon which so much hinges as the cardinal nation of the United Kingdom Federation.

## Free England: the liberal geography of our
### prosperous present

Where is this England? Where are its boundaries? What shape will Free England assume within the United Kingdom Federation? Where does England's vital centre live? Conventional maps of the result of the 2016 referendum make the Remain communities and constituencies appear scattered and diminished when compared with the misleadingly expansive reach of Leave England. Remain Wales faces a similar challenge of geographic disparity: the communities of west Wales, such as Ceredigion and Gwynedd, that backed Remain seem as far away from the Remain heartland anchored in Cardiff, Monmouth and the Vale of Glamorgan as the apparently isolated areas of northern England, such as Manchester and Liverpool, that voted with Remain London, seem from the capital so far to the south. Think of Exeter, which chose to remain in the EU while much of the rural West Country supported Leave; or Newcastle, which also (narrowly) supported Remain, in the face of large Leave majorities in much of rural and suburban north-east England.

The conventional mapping of the results of the 2016 referendum is a cartographical deception. It encourages the Leave supporter to overestimate the extent and importance of Brexit Britain. We know that such maps unwisely disguise the imbalance in the power relationship between the dynamic and wealthier areas of Remain England and the ageing and economically moribund regions of the English Leaver. These unrepresentative maps form part of the mental furniture we must discard if we are to make a success of the United Kingdom Federation.

The map of mind that matters most is the splendid urban array of energetic English cities that stretches from north to south, from beneath Hadrian's Wall to the English Channel, from Newcastle and Leeds to Brighton and Hove. A majority of the men and women who constitute our vital centre make their homes in the economic hothouses of Remain England. These great English cities are united in profitable business dynamism and enlightened political culture with the majority Remain-voting cities of Northern Ireland (Belfast), Scotland (Glasgow, Edinburgh and Aberdeen) and Wales (Cardiff, and probably Swansea now). As a web nation, Remain England now has a technological infrastructure that complements the road, rail and air links that fed the growth and vitality of all these cities. In turn, Free England and Free Wales offer an instructively brusque meditation on the unequal fortunes of our less prosperous towns versus our more successful cities.

## TOWN VERSUS CITY: THE PLACE TO BE YOUNG IS THE PLACE TO GROW OLD

How is one to explain the deep and growing gap between the economic productivity and wealth of Remain cities when contrasted with the stagnant and sullen towns of Little England? For a variety of complex reasons with which economists and sociologists continue to wrestle, too many English towns have found it difficult to exploit the growth potential of globalization, and therefore have often appeared to be, and consequently feel that they have been, left behind by the surging cities that may be located quite nearby. Take, for example, Reading versus Swindon, or Norwich versus Great Yarmouth, or Nottingham versus Barnsley, or Bristol versus Weston-super-Mare. The relevant Welsh analogy might be Cardiff compared to Newport (or, more painful still, my father's family home town of Pontypridd).

The referendum result cast into sharp relief the complex truth that English cities have thrived on the four freedoms of our membership of the European single market. In contrast, many English towns have proven unable or unwilling to work the requisite magic of the economic miracle they must perform on themselves if they are to flourish in the twenty-first century. In short, where once, before the referendum, Leave voters in England saw our great multicultural cities as a threat to their towns and their pristine English 'whiteness', now the perception has been reversed, because the Remain voter (rightly in my view) fears that the resentful inhabitants of Leave's failing towns are demanding policies that threaten the prosperity of our most productive urban centres.

Partition respects this fateful division of mind. The realistic divorce of Remain and Leave nations would ease the dangers in both directions, encouraging our prosperous cities, like Singapore, to continue on their globalizing path to massive wealth creation while allowing the most frightened and vengeful of our towns and villages to revert to the economic rhythms, modest means, and ethno-racial purity of England as it was in the 1950s and 1960s, before we joined the European Economic Community and before the 'Big Bang' reforms of Thatcherism. The hidden premise of the partition argument is stark: to undermine London will not rescue Grimsby; it will just ensure the diminishment of both communities, and to no humane purpose whatever.

To acknowledge that hidden premise is to lend still more weight to the argument for partition. Think how often journalists have concluded from their analyses of voter intentions since June 2016 that the Brexit supporter is completely sanguine about the dangers of bringing down the temple of British prosperity in an economically destructive act to drive out 'Johnny Foreigner'. Unlike some advocates of a second referendum who bank on a change of heart, the proponent of partition insists that such destructive indifference is sincere, the stuff of the deeply held conviction of many Leave voters that immigrants of any colour have no place in English life.

Finally, as the Welsh realist advocate of partition would argue, we must accept Leavers as they are. We can take them seriously by listening to them with our full attention. And, having done so, and only after having done so, we must, if necessary, abandon them. Only partition will free the UK's vital centre from the literally unbearable economic baggage of the Brexiteer, his bare pockets and her empty purse filled only with resentment, and despondency mixed with contempt for the energy and discipline that proper capitalism demands.

In essence, the Leaver represents an economic deadweight. We Remainers cannot carry you because we don't have the means. Furthermore, the Brexiteer poses a profound menace to what economic means we actually do have. Let us press home this argument: there is no point in our trying to save you if you will barely lift a finger to save yourselves. To this point Thatcher's belligerent war cry, 'No, no, no', is not an answer. I will push this assessment to its uncomfortably brutal but also realistic conclusion in the final chapter of this essay.

BORE DA!

The United Kingdom Federation will provide the indispensable fortress for our great centres of wealth creation today and tomorrow. The instinctive preference of many Jews and most gays for living in the centres of our larger cities points a prophetic finger at the ruling ideology of early twenty-first-century happiness: triumphant urbanism. At its most compelling and therefore most persuasive, Free England stands as the definitive rejection of the nineteenth- and early twentieth-century cults of anti-urbanism. In this sense, Samuel Johnson, that forceful eighteenth-century urbanite, was right: 'When a man is tired of London, he is tired of life': but this witticism – and this is the glory of the thing – does not apply only to London now.

Much of what will be the UKF is already united by the conviction that life is best lived in a comfortable apartment with a handsome balcony looking out on a vibrant agora and beyond, housed in a great city with its piazzas, malls, theatres and stadiums, home to the public spaces where today we live our lives in Latin fashion, in the street and in happy sight of each other. How else does one explain the joyous exuberance (and, yes, excesses) of the clubs, bars, cafés and restaurants of our great cities? Dubliners can readily appreciate the point. Think of the good-tempered chaos of the streets and footpaths of Temple Bar on a liquid Good Friday.

Granted, many of our young people are still battling to break free of the inhibiting rictus of that Victorian value, secretive privacy. Purged by their drunken excesses, they, too, will be, as they mature, converted to the civilizing pleasures of what Italians call *il cuore della città* ('the heart of the city'). Like Italian footballers in the beautifully tailored suits they sport when in the in public eye, our young will be seduced by the joys of civilized display, the confident grace of good manners, and the sexy elegance of the *bella figura* one finds impressively displayed by so many straight Cardiffian men in their forties and fifties – indeed, by all those subtle ingredients that our aristocratic forebears believed so enhanced the enduring satisfactions of good adult company.

This new cult of urbanism has transformed rural England into a sphere of rest and renewal for the busy, successful urbanite, who finds the notion of escaping from the city to retire in genteel poverty as at once odd and unattractive. The magnetic field that once made rural Cowbridge, to cite a Welsh example, seem a more civilized place to grow old than the creative Cardiff that stretches from Pontcanna and Cardiff Bay has now been reversed; today the draw is to the Welsh capital, just as on the national scale, the draw is to London.

The only exception may be the burnt-out Londoner who has overdosed on financial market adrenaline; but even this victim who retreats to the countryside embodies a form of urban pastoralism that no rural community shares. Furthermore, our cities are where we all need to return when we decide to stop driving and start walking, to downsize our possessions and the domestic space needed to house them, and to celebrate anew the comforting virtues of urban life with its efficient systems of transport, enhanced shopping opportunities, better cultural and sporting amenities and superior health care. This truth provides the other rider to Johnson's quip.

For the old faced with eventual infirmity and contracting horizons, the well-organized British city offers a comforting miracle, because during the decades after retirement you need to get out of your car and walk to stay active and mobile in order to fight the great plagues of old age in the Leave Nations: obesity and loneliness. In the light of this imperative, it makes sense to call to mind all the English equivalents of the urban sophistication and 'get-up-and-go' of the friendly neighbourhoods of Cardiff Bay. Here one can walk safely in under ten minutes – Cardiff Central and John Lewis take about twenty – to the GP's surgery, the dentist, the chemist, the post office, a selection of shops, an impressive choice of cafés, bars and restaurants, to say nothing of the Welsh Millennium Centre and other first-class entertainment venues, while being in easy reach by bus or taxi of Wales's largest hospital and busiest international airport.

In all these ways, life in urban Britain trumps the undeniable charms of living in our countryside. At their best, the apartment complexes of our major cities – and this is definitely true of Greater Cardiff – can be triumphs of stimulating vitality, intergenerational mutual aid and age-indifferent solidarity. Sometimes one feels, probably unfairly, that the people in the Leave nations tend to come across as boring, old and grumpy because all their fun neighbours have already escaped to Remain Britain. Such are the pleasures of Britain's vital centre. All one needs to do is to keep one's financial wits about one (but that is necessary everywhere and always).

Certainly, the range of expertise, experience and youthful energy on tap in the medium-build estates populated by Remain urbanites is unrivalled. It is invigorating and encouraging to be surrounded by young people. Furthermore, we city dwellers, particularly in the provinces, have the time to take care of ourselves and look after each other. This is another of those Welsh urges that should not be confined to urban Wales; the Londoner commuter uneasy with strangers who say 'good morning' should spend some time in Cardiff Bay.

THE URBAN MARCHES

Now let us populate the map of the United Kingdom Federation with the roll of honour of our always lively but also often splendid urban sanctuaries. Outside the capital, this includes all the English cities that voted against Brexit. Think of the conurbations along the M6 and M4: Manchester, Liverpool and Bristol voted by clear majorities to Remain. Leeds voted by a hair to remain; Birmingham by a slight margin to Leave. I think that Remain England offers the logical economic home for Leeds and Birmingham; but, consistent with the principle that the referendum result be used to draw the boundaries between the United Kingdom Federation and the Kingdom of England, it is assumed here that Leeds will be part of the UKF and Birmingham part of the KE. As for Milton Keynes, I find it impossible to understand why this extraordinarily go-ahead city voted for Brexit, albeit by a smallish margin.

To this long list of Remain cities should be added England's university centres, beginning with Oxford, Cambridge and Bath (one of the rare cities that voted to betray its university by voting for Leave was Durham), as well as such fintech, venture capital and technology hubs such as Reading and Newbury. So Free England is formed from an alliance of 'connect-the-dots' cities linked and energized by technology, modern transport and free markets for international capital and pan-European labour. All these communities would suffer significant damage, immediate or long-term, if they were no longer part of the European Union, and that is why they voted to remain. The fact that the English and Welsh Brexiteer appears to be indifferent to his or her own economic interest baffles Remainers: we know how to add and subtract our pounds and euros, but we are not so sure you do.

For the economist, the cosmopolitan mega-city allied with a constellation of dispersed smaller urban centres constitutes a new kind of state/nation/economy. Our mega-cities are twentieth-century concepts and twenty-first-century facts of life. The Remainer accepts the reality of this invention, while the Leaver, like King Canute, wants to fight it. In any case, the nineteenth-century notion of a nation-state consisting of a large contiguous territory uniting a population that shares one culture, religion, race, language and royal house was under siege even before the First World War. The Holocaust was a terrifying reaction against the cosmopolitan modernity of tolerance, diversity and democracy that blossomed after the peace of Versailles in 1920. Contrary to the Brexit faith, this modernity was and is not responsible for such illiberal horrors: it is the psychologically insecure hater, the rabid ethnic cleanser and the 'blood and soil' ideologue who were and are to blame. One must be clear here about who did what to whom, and who would do what to whom now.

## PASSPORTS, BLACK AND WHITE: HOW FREE ENGLAND WILL WORK

Toll bridges and local customs unions were a significant feature of the economies of early modern Europe, but giant cities as free-standing political communities will strike many people today as an almost medieval concept. The idea of Greater Manchester and Greater Bristol as the political building blocks of a Free England may remind movie buffs of *Passport to Pimlico*. But the comparison soon breaks, down because these conurbations of northern and western England are vastly larger than the microdot-sized Duchy of Burgundy of the celebrated Ealing comedy. Size matters. And so does the *élan vital* of our army of urban millions.

The Remainer city dweller delights in the always diverting, always stimulating, always-something-new diversity and bustle of our great urban centres, but the scale and drive of our cities often make the timid Leaver nervous and suspicious. She finds the concrete labyrinths and complex warrens of our great cities unfamiliar, even threatening. (What such faint-hearted souls from Bourton-on-the Water, Dulverton, Blackwater or Gorleston on Sea, for example, would make of truly vast megacities, such as Tokyo, Shanghai or Bangkok, I cannot imagine.) And this returns us to our central conundrum.

If this division of mind between the economically defeated Brexiteer and the confident pro-European globalizer is so profound as to block a ready ballot-box cure, we arrive, once more, at our unavoidable conclusion: a Free England can grow and prosper only if cut loose from this resentful, xenophobic and reactionary hinterland inhabited by these self-isolating and fearful people who appear to be at once unnerved by change and growth and simultaneously so contemptuous of foreigners that they want either to expel them or to applaud violence against them. To repeat the point: a fruitful communal life cannot be shared with such people.

In short, Brexit has brutally exposed the limitations of the old-fashioned contiguous nation-state. This notion of the nation stands in need of radical refashioning if it is to meet our continental- and global-scale economic needs. Might we not require, therefore, the more imaginative approach to the organization of the urban economy that is already embodied in the Remain nations? In this respect, it is comforting to realize that our medieval ancestors who lived in Venice or Amsterdam or any Hanseatic League town (Lübeck, for example) would have no difficulty appreciating the fact that the power and influence of our centres of talent and energy are dispersed and scattered across the map of our national geography.

'Unfurl the sails!' is the battle cry of the dynamic Remainer community. Living as they did in a world of peasants bound to somebody's else fields, any of those mobile medieval urbanites – think of Thomas More or Marco Polo, Erasmus or Columbus – would readily understand how these dispersed centres might share so much with other such centres, and therefore how they might be organically more tightly linked by closeness of mind to such centres, however geographically distant, than to the resentful and uncomprehending hinterlands often no more than ten kilometres away.

If Greater Manchester, Liverpool and Bristol as component parts of the UKF will, in effect, become wealthy, multicultural urban islands surrounded by the cold, hostile and impoverished seas of Leave England, how should we imagine the suburban and rural hinterlands that separate, say, Liverpool from Birmingham? In *Wayward Pines*, an American sci-fi television series that benefits from British acting talent, a dystopia composed of an isolated community of more or less healthy human beings is confined within a walled community surrounded by a vast territory abandoned to the descendants of a nuclear holocaust (mutants or 'Abbies'). I am not suggesting Leavers are 'Abbies'. Quite the contrary: the point of this analogy is to stretch our imaginations around our new post-referendum geographical realities, not further inflame Leave feelings.

For a more sober, less futuristic analogy, recall the real-world example of West Berlin during the Cold War. Occupied and administered by three of the four great power victors of the Second World War, West Berlin was isolated within the large expanse of East Germany, connected to West Germany by walled and patrolled autobahns that kept West Germans from entering East Germany, and East Germans from escaping to the West. But for the potential of technology and what I call 'black passporting', our new schoolroom maps of Remain and Leave England might have ended up looking like a postmodern version of East Germany, fittingly furnished with convenient branches of Aldi and Lidl – but only in the Remain Nations.

True, the fictional examples of *Passport to Pimlico* and *Wayward Pines* and the factual example of West Berlin during the Cold War offer three visions of urban exclusion. In their contrasting ways, they conjure a picture of what the main cities of England would look like if they were nothing more than vast gated communities, twenty-first-century versions of West Berlin surrounded by another country: not East Germany but Leave Britain. This is not what I am proposing, because there would be no physical walls dividing Leave England from Remain England. Rather, a form of what might be called 'black passporting' (whereby the foreigner's passport is blacked out) would serve to keep the territory of Leave England, the Kingdom of England, free of outsiders. This technological fix would secure another perfect British compromise: a welcome army of foreign university students for the Remain nations, and batches of cheap American-made genetically altered junk food for the Leavers (the full 'Abbie' breakfast); something for everyone. Or everyone, that is, until the very minute when we begin to care about what we feed our children.

Using the technological control that banks already exercise over the credit-card user, only citizens of the Kingdom of England (Brexit Land) would have an electronic passport that would allow them to pay for food, fuel or shelter within the Kingdom. Access to banking facilities and the NHS, and the purchase or renting of property, would be electronically impossible for non-citizens of the Kingdom of England. Johnny Foreigner would be able to drive across Leave England, fly into one its airports or use its train network; but he or she would be unable to stay or live or work in Leave England because every official transaction or legal payment would require a native passport. The practical limitations and merits of black passporting will be addressed in Chapter 7 below on the ethnic cleansing of Little England, but the principal gain would be that the threat of immigration, and the affront of outsiders living, working and speaking Polish, Romanian or Welsh that so upsets the Leave voter, would thereby be all but totally eliminated. Johnny Foreigner as residential irritation or threat would be banished for good.

Observe how such a system would permit any citizen of the United Kingdom Federation to drive, fly or travel by train from London to Manchester with complete freedom as long as that traveller did not attempt to buy any service or product or stay in the Kingdom of England (aside from motorway pit stops and the like). Furthermore, all of Free England's supply chains and shipping routes, from, say, Dover to Edinburgh, would be open but secure in ways that would leave the Kingdom of England safe and undisturbed in its isolation. The vast army of lorries and trucks that, as noted above, pour into Britain from the continent every day would therefore be able to travel the length and breadth of the successor states of the old United Kingdom hampered only by the limited black passporting inconveniences noted. Nissan's giant plant in Sunderland would be linked to the UKF in every direction necessary by secure transport corridors. We owe this much to the Japanese investors. After all, they trusted us to secure their logistical and marketing access from England and Wales to the rest of the EU. It will be the task of the UKF to repay this debt of trust that the Leave nations now refuse to honour.

Blacking out foreign passports is a harsh and blunt method of securing the physical openness of the borders between the Leave and Remain nations, but it would ensure that Free England prospers, and the United Kingdom Federation with it. Note, however, that black passporting does not offer a persuasive fix for the Brexiteer plans, at once superficial, ill-conceived and even dangerous, for Northern Ireland. More important than the untested and very expensive technology itself is the motive behind the Brexiteer's weakness for half-baked technical solutions to complex problems. The saving grace in all this is that, as part of the United Kingdom Federation, Northern Ireland would not need any form of black passporting except as a bar to people, goods, services and money from the now closed Kingdom of England. Will the Brexit voting constituencies that return Democratic Unionist Members of Parliament really want to be a part of this closed state, or what the Japanese call *sakoku?* Partition would force the answer.

At the most profound level, the open-minded cosmopolitan liberal cannot share a country with her closed-minded nationalist cousin for reasons that can only be described as philosophical. At root, we are talking about our metaphysical assumptions about reality: facts, hypotheses, objectivity, scientific truth, the mind and, finally and most influentially, the nature of 'the other': other cultures, other languages, other people. The implied divide between the mental world of most Celts and most Little English is nearly fatal at almost every level. Yet, most intriguing of all, the majority of English Remainers have managed to break free of the perverse shallows of so-called 'English philosophy'.

So, in addition to all the rest, there are decisive philosophical reasons, English and Celtic, why we must examine our governing assumptions about what political reality is and how we are to shape it in a more humane fashion. Only then will we be able to explain how the Welsh realist has managed to evade the blow that H. L. Mencken struck against the superficial Anglo-American belief that only the immediately obvious is true when he observed that 'For every complex problem, there is an answer that is clear, simple and wrong.' Here, once again, contrary to Little English metaphysics (the vulgar abuse of 'Occam's razor'), we must pursue the facts of the matter of Brexit guided by the Celtic perception that truth often resides beneath the obscuring fog of a mere surface. Some problems are complex. Some truths are deep. Welcome to a different kind of metaphysics, and therefore a different approach to political identity. Welcome to Ireland.

CHAPTER 5

# No more Troubles: a new partition of the UK as the practical answer to the Irish Question

*To put it bluntly, Ireland has evolved a complex and fluid sense of what it means to have a national identity while England has reverted to a simplistic and static one. This fault line opens a crack into which the whole Brexit project may stumble.*

— *FINTAN O'TOOLE*[1]

## PART I – MORE THAN ONE THING

### SINGING GRAVEL

LET US BEGIN WITH TWO vignettes on the Irish question from academic life: first a dispiriting backward-looking glance, then a very different tale ripe with the future. One of the innovations of modern British academe is the external examiner who does not examine as such but who assesses the fairness and accuracy of examination markings by this or that teaching department. To get a better understanding of the function of the external examiner I approached a colleague in a prestigious faculty of another Welsh university who had served as an external examiner for one of Northern Ireland's centres of higher learning that I had been encouraged to admire. His remarks were nuanced and useful, but when he completed his explanation, he said: 'Of course, Wales is a different country.'

---

[1] 'Brexit's Irish Question', *New York Review of Books*, September 28, 2017.

Sensing my perplexity at this comment, he told this worn-leather of a story. One Northern Irish student had achieved a result just one point short of a first class in his fourth-year finals. When the marks were adjudicated, my Welsh colleague kindly suggested that it would be churlish not to raise the mark by a single point to give the young man a first; he had done that well. This proposal, conventional in its orthodoxy, was promptly rejected by the committee – but to humble an external examiner in this way may be risky, because he or she submits a formal official statement on the adjudication process. So this Welshman was taken aside after the meeting and told: 'We couldn't possibly award a first to that student; he's a Catholic.' All this was six or seven years *after* the Good Friday Agreement. Can you imagine this happening, then or now, at Oxford or UCLA, Heidelberg or Swansea?

My other vignette is as fresh as tomorrow morning in its arresting novelty. About the same time as I was learning how the politics of undergraduate examination markings worked in Northern Ireland, I had the opportunity, quite by chance, to teach something rarely taught in Wales: a university course on Middle Eastern politics. The first day I arrived to lecture, only to discover something I have previously never encountered in my very ethnically diverse home faculty: a class consisting almost entirely of a small sea of white west European faces. The two ethnic exceptions were interesting. One was a bright, self-possessed Palestinian student who had experience of Arab–Israeli youth congresses and the like. I made him my informal class assistant (none of the other students had been to the Holy Land or knew Arabic or Hebrew). Together we worked through the course reading list methodically and fairly. My set texts included a volume by a Harvard law professor, Alan Dershowitz's *The Case for Israel*. My Palestinian student made, as I knew he would, a good fist of it.

My students were not sympathetic to Dershowitz's arguments, but I thought it was essential that they spend some time perusing a considered position with which they might not agree. This gesture towards Welsh realism, this all but irresistible because inbred urge towards objectivity, was overshadowed metaphysically by the one unambiguously non-white student in the class. His face was east Asian, but in our complex world it is usually wiser to assume nothing, so I tentatively asked where he was from. To which he forthrightly replied: 'I'm from Northern Ireland.'

The sound he made when he spoke was the 'singing gravel' of a perfect Belfast accent. The juxtaposition of face and voice was uncanny. It called into doubt all and any superficial assumptions about what it means to be 'Northern Irish' or 'Irish' or 'British' or 'Catholic' or 'Protestant'. Was he a UK-born Chinese–Irish citizen of Belfast who might also be a dutiful Confucian or practising Buddhist? Was he any or all or none of the above? Or was 'or' the wrong word here, 'and' the better one?

Whatever the answer, it had to be more than one thing because he was more than one thing, and only he could tell us which of those more than one things he was. Such acts of contemporary self-definition thrust us, as we shall see, into the very heart of the newness of our newly reborn Ireland. These considerations put us on the approaches to the subtle post-essentialist frontier of mind that today separates not the North of Ireland from the South, but the better part of Ireland from Leave Britain. This is the revolutionary mental border over which the Brexiteer may yet fatally stumble.

THE ENGLISH QUESTION AND THE IRISH ANSWER

After partition, what would be the geographical character of the four Remain nations, including Northern Ireland? Each country would be best understood not as a leaden, fixed place or a swatch of colour on a map, but as a great national project: a community going somewhere, always self-transforming: diversity united by a shared purpose. National identities in these four projects – English,

Irish, Scottish and Welsh – would be plural, flexible and ambiguous, and therefore neither 'static' nor 'simplistic'. Borders would be kept and respected, but never allowed to impede our economic advance or a plural sense of self. This postmodern flexible sense of political identity on a national scale is an Irish invention, and this essay could not have been written without the politically fluid and polysemic pronouns ('we' and 'I' and the rest) literally underwritten by this Irish innovation.

In my schema for the first partition of the islands since 1922, Northern Ireland would become a self-governing nation as part of the United Kingdom Federation. As a member of the European Union, the UKF would have an open border with the Republic of Ireland, just as it does today. This would protect the vulnerable peace of Northern Ireland from the retrograde dangers of 'take back control' English nationalism. At the same time, 'Orange' Protestant anxieties would be eased (there is no cure) by securing Northern Ireland firmly within the larger political community of the United Kingdom Federation. Furthermore, those Northern Ireland communities that voted for Brexit might become detached parts of the Kingdom of England, though this would need careful thought. Chapter 7 below, on England, examines some of the ideas, mechanisms and technology necessary for such Brexit-mandated detachments. Chapter 6 below, on Scotland, wrestles with the reverse proposition: how to address the tensions between independence for a unitary state and the Leave–Remain divide within a single but still divided nation.

Partition and the birth of the United Kingdom Federation would help to soothe the irritants that exacerbate the paralytic sectarian standoff between Sinn Fein and its Protestant political opponents in five ways unmatched by any alternative 'solution' to the Brexiteer's Irish problem. First, the economic threat to both the Irish Republic and Northern Ireland would be largely averted because the Republic, as a member of the European Union, would retain frictionless trade access to the North and to the more dynamic and much the larger part of the British mainland economy. Second, the customs border and single market demarcation between the Kingdom of England and all of Ireland as well as the rest of the European Union would be redrawn deep into English and Welsh territory, thus eliminating the contentious issue of border controls between the Republic and Northern Ireland as well as the need for a sea border between the islands of Ireland and Britain.

Third, as noted above, partition would preserve all the achievements of the Treaty of Belfast (the Good Friday Agreement) while also offering practical encouragement for the end of direct rule from Westminster. In short, the advocate of partition wants to secure the conditions for effective, inclusive government from Stormont by making tribal intransigence seem just that much more irrelevant to Irish realities and therefore allowing Northern Ireland to adopt just that much more of a position of detente. Fourth, as a realistic backstop in the meantime, while we encourage this still deeper relaxation of the old tribal divisions, a select handful of essential decisions about the Northern Irish economy and society as a whole, as part of the United Kingdom Federation, would be taken, as now, in London and Brussels as well as Belfast.

Fifth (in tandem with the fourth), the United Kingdom Federation would provide a sheet anchor for Northern Ireland. When necessity demanded action, the UKF could exercise the powers and responsibilities of direct rule from London as a *temporary* fix for what must be a temporary problem. In the long term or the short, Northern Ireland must master the art of post-sectarian self-government as an essential act of mental decolonization. Nowhere else in the United Kingdom will this rebirth of collective, because shared, Irish self-mastery elicit more interest and sympathy than in Wales, where we are proceeding down the same decolonizing road (with different potholes).

This transitional ambition on the way to the ultimate goal would be realized with a Northern Ireland that would be capable of making its way in the world by paying its way. It would also need to be able to contribute, such are the dangers that now threaten Europe, to the collective defence of the UKF and the European Union as a whole. On this sensitive subject, we might affirm that the traditional Irish preference for insular non-alignment and strict pacifism would be stroked, watered, fed – and transmuted; ourselves alone no more.

A Northern Ireland that could serve the collective defence of our continent in this way must be able to govern itself. In such a constitutional arrangement, the bond between the Republic and a reimagined Northern Ireland would be economically seamless, culturally intimate and politically unbreakable. The potentially detached Brexit-voting constituencies aside, Ireland would become a unity, at one with itself; quietly, pervasively and uncontentiously one. In this spirit and this manner, when formal unity finally returns to the island of Ireland, it will arrive like a gentle Irish spring under the friendly banner of an old Latin tag: *E pluribus unum*.

## PART II - THE EUROPEAN ENLIGHTENMENT AND THE NEW IRELAND
### ADAM SMITH AND VOLTAIRE

During the past two decades or so, the Irish have transformed themselves. Close observers of the national scene such as Fintan O'Toole of *The Irish Times* identify three key changes: the decline of the clerical authority of the Roman Catholic Church; the transformation of the Irish economy, as part of the European Union, by the powers of globalization; and the reinvention of the Irish sense of nationhood. I agree with this assessment, and will seek to deepen our appreciation of this remarkable metamorphosis by focusing on just two cardinal ideas from the European Enlightenment that are so vital to this Irish transformation: Adam Smith's concept of market forces and, in passing, Voltaire's insistence that we shatter the prestige of organized religion.

In this section, I will expand on Adam Smith's notion of economic markets, as shaped by hands visible and invisible, and enquire what this fruitful and rational notion means today to Ireland (as well as to the Remain and Leave nations); but first a brief word on Voltaire. If this witty eighteenth-century French *philosophe* and scourge of Roman Catholicism were living now and visited Ireland, he would ask: 'Is your country a modern, enlightened society?' We would respond 'Definitely,' citing the referendum votes to decriminalize homosexuality and overturn the constitutional ban on abortion. We would hail the triumph of Irish liberal-mindedness embodied in a Taoiseach who is openly gay and ethnically part Indian.

In response, Voltaire would nod in approval, but those sharp intelligent eyes would hold our glance for a moment. And because French gentleness was only a part of the man, he would then press an unsparing question on us: 'Have you crushed the infamous thing?' (*Avez-vous écrasé l'infâme?*). We need to address what Voltaire meant by this, in an Irish Catholic context, and how it relates to his kindlier other half as a person; but these considerations will take on their full liberating implications only when we have brooded first on the link between the rational free market and the Irish deconstruction of ethnic nationalism. So, for the moment, you may stop fumbling nervously with the rosary still secreted in your pocket until we are prepared to return Voltaire's unnerving smile. This we must learn to do in another time and place. Here, economics and nationalism will dominate our concerns.

ECONOMIC BORDERS HARD AND SOFT

*The Wealth of Nations*, Adam Smith's master demonstration of the powers of the factually enquiring and rational mind, famously appeared in 1776, the same year as America's Declaration of Independence from Britain. The very pages of the book are redolent with the air of intellectual freedom and self-mastery. In this classic work, one of the most influential books ever penned in the Celtic Fringe, Smith insisted that the invisible workings of economic markets enrich us all. To be part of a dynamic marketplace, the larger the better, is to ensure the potential for an enhanced material quality of life for every family of every businessman or woman who can raise his or her game and compete. The European single market, like the North American Free Trade Agreement, is such an economic cash machine, and Ireland has exploited to the full the opportunities that have come its way via the single market. Such exploitation demanded the unresisting embrace of the free movement of capital, people, goods and (someday soon) services.

The faltering response of Trump's America and Brexit Britain to the power and potential of vast regional markets on a continental scale (where populations are measured in the hundreds of millions), such as the European single market as regulated by the European Commission and the European Court of Justice, has been feeble and incoherent by the intellectual standards of the Republic of Ireland. Often regarded by many educated Englishmen and women as hopelessly romantic and muddled about the demands of modern life, the Celts are, on this subject today, clear and unmoveable. We know how to butter our bread. Do you?

The vexed topic of economic borders explains this otherwise inexplicable contrast between the Remain and Leave nations. The Brexiteer's call for 'taking back control' harks back to the nineteenth-century nationalist commitment to strict borders, the more rigid and bloodily defended the better. During the twentieth century, the growth of regional economies, connected by border-transcending infrastructural systems such as railways and power grids, called this rigidity into doubt. When, in the 1930s, economic nationalists, the spiritual ancestors of the Brexiteers, tried to take back control by ignoring the new reality and importance of pan-European region-wide economies of scale, the consequences were higher unemployment, lower economic growth and, finally, a set of conflicts over borders that morphed into total war.

This, in essence, was the central warning of Lord Keynes's 1919 book *The Economic Consequences of the Peace*, perhaps the most famous and most thoughtful response to the disaster of the Great War and its cataclysmic economic aftermath. Keynes prophetically warned that if politicians and diplomats decided to force the contraction of the German economy in a Europe where so many countries depended on German economic vitality and growth, then everyone was going to suffer. And so we did.

A hundred years out of date, the hard Brexiteer's indifference to the importance of border-transcending supply chains to the success, indeed viability, of British manufacturing, for example, reflects the same punishing illogic that informed the disastrous economic impact of the lost peace after Versailles. Today, the Brexiteer wants to constrict the enormous tidal flows of commerce that now surge freely across national borders within the European single market; but such 'beggar-thy-neighbour' policies will be punished by market forces just as the market punished so much of Europe after the First World War. In terms of market energy, the whole of Ireland is a unity, and the Brexiteer would be wise to respect this fact – or leave it to the Remain nations to nurture the economic integration and solidarity of the United Kingdom Federation by building on such facts.

CHEESE WARS: A WELSH DIGRESSION (SUBSTITUTE IRISH EXAMPLES WHERE RELEVANT)

The malign character of 'beggar-thy-neighbour' economic irrationalism is easy to illustrate. Let us take the British and Irish passion for cheese. I love cheese, and when I first moved into Cardiff

I became a customer of one of the Welsh capital's oldest cheese-mongers. The business attracted my custom because it marketed a select but still attractive range of European fine foods. Then the shop's owners decided to cut back on French and Italian speciality items in favour of Welsh products that were similar but not quite in the same class in terms of quality. No Irish butter was on offer for like reasons.

When I queried the new policy, the owner told me that he had decided that in order to support Welsh products it was necessary to eliminate foreign competition from the shelves. This argument has great instinctual appeal but it is not sound economics (unless you are Japanese or Friedrich List). In the 1930s, in the name of protecting local industries and producers, trade barriers went up across Europe and the British Empire, with disastrous consequences. Any introductory economics textbook will provide a summary of the brilliant insights modern economists from Adam Smith onwards have brought to bear on the false 'choice' between local and foreign products.

It barely touches on the depth of these economic ideas to suggest that superior foreign imports stimulate the improvement of home brands, in both cost and quality. Furthermore, expanding one's market to include not only Wales and Britain but all of Europe offers much greater economic rewards in the form of much increased profits. The trick is to welcome French products to Wales and to encourage the French to sell quality Welsh products in France, a nation of demanding consumers of food and drink. So one can now buy upmarket Welsh spring water at places such as Paris's Charles de Gaulle Airport, where the whole world can sample it, and therefore buy it. Why confine your wares to a market of three million Welsh people when you have unrestricted access to the EU market of nearly five hundred million? One must, quite simply, aim higher. As the Irish already do.

I uncovered a still more depressing example of the same kind of error on a more recent shopping expedition. I came across another cheese merchant in one of our traditional covered markets, someone who had taken real trouble with his shop design in the cheese-mad Welsh capital. When I decided to sample his goods, I asked whether he sold pecorino or brie as well as Somerset cheddar and Welsh *y fenni*. To which he responded that he sold only *British* cheese. Properly done, such a niche marketing strategy might succeed; but my question obviously irritated the cheesemonger, who went on to declare in a rather offended manner that Britain had no need for foreign cheese. I then gently reminded him that Cardiff is Remain country, and the very idea of refusing to eat foreign cheese because it was foreign cuts no ice here. We think this attitude is risible. Nevertheless, to close our encounter on an even keel I bought a sample of his recommended English cheese. It wasn't the best.

The problem of economic nationalism transcends cheese. These days, at peak hours for electrical consumption (teatime and whenever the FA cup final is on the television are the old measures), the British national grid depends on supplementary power supplies from the French national grid. This very prudent solution to a practical problem makes the Brexiteer reach for his pistol, while the soft borderist (the Remainer, for example) is entirely sanguine about such dependence because 'taking back control' in such circumstances is commercial nonsense. The confident rejection of border controls over the very large flows of trade between Northern Ireland and the Republic reflects the same sensible economic approach.

A MATTER OF SIZE
Ultimately, the border question is about something much larger: the unique power of free markets that benefit from the free

movement of people on a continental scale, and how all Europeans profit from this 'scale merit'. From the viewpoint of the economist, borders are lines drawn around markets and spheres of regulatory responsibility. For the proponent of 'scale merit', the logic of the thing is simple: the larger the market the better. So what does 'scale merit' mean in plain English? It works this way. The larger the market, the more you can sell. The more you can sell, the more you can produce. The more you produce, the cheaper the costs of production become. The larger the market, the larger the potential return on every euro, pound or dollar invested. The larger the market, the larger your potential pool of talented and motivated people from which to hire. The larger the market, the larger the amount of capital there is for investment. And so on. Now imagine this logic at work every day in thousands of businesses across the European Union, and try to estimate in your mind the massive benefits that result.

Because size matters in this way, all rational arguments about British membership of the European Union, as embodied, in this case, by the single market, should begin with the recognition of how lucky we are to belong to so vast a market – the world's largest. Can free markets, however large, be improved? Certainly, they can. In so complex a human institution as the single market, there is always (and will always be) scope for improvements, small and large; but scale merit is so enriching that it can never be trumped by regulatory inefficiency or poor business practice, and this is because the gains from continental-sized economies of scale almost always outweigh any such economic defect, real or imagined.

The intellectual consequences of this truth are telling and straightforward. The single market is so large, so intrinsically efficient (the 'Adam Smith' effect), that no economically literate person would ever argue for leaving a market this big, and this well-regulated, because of secondary complaints about 'red tape', 'bureaucracy' or 'business-restrictive cartels'. It is not that such criticisms are necessarily invalid; simply that they are not anything like as important as the would-be critic of the single market assumes. Thus, to reinforce the point, the practical person would strive endlessly to improve the single market in all kinds of ways but would never dream of abandoning it. That would be irrational because economically self-harming. In the language of pub talk, be it in suburban Cleveland or rural Devon, the very idea of Britain leaving the single market is simply stupid. Why? Because we know the gains from leaving so large a single market will never outweigh the benefits of belonging to it, and this remains true whether the single market sails under the flag of the European Union or not. QED.

THE EU AS A REGULATORY SUPERPOWER

In pursuit of balance, let us consider an alternative but very well-informed perspective on the secondary but vital issue of regulatory competence over a large continental-sized market, in this case the EU itself. Here is an excerpt from a speech recently delivered at the University of Glasgow by Sir Ivan Roger's, the former UK ambassador to the European Union:

> No single post-Brexit model will work for all. But if we want, in [many or all] areas, genuinely to go it alone – or have to, because we cannot accept the jurisdictional and dispute resolution implications of staying in agencies run at the EU level in which our voice is lessened – then we have to be going full tilt in developing that regulatory capability at huge speed, rather than assuming the EU is bound to give us both associate membership and a serious role from outside its policy setting, when the only way that can happen is if we shift our red line on jurisdiction questions.
>
> That was promulgated as a red line [by the UK government] when no serious thought at all had been given

to these questions.The fact that, in so many areas, we are obviously NOT doing that, and both regulators and industries are making it clear that they have no intention of replicating, at great cost, regulatory capability which already exists, is yet another reason why the EU side has long since concluded that the UK would not walk out.

Because it could not.

No amount of 'be careful: we could still walk out, you know' sabre rattling makes the slightest odds when the other side knows that the day after doing so, we would be back pleading for continuity and for the on-going delivery of, and access to, functions the British State has no capability to provide.[2]

Thus Sir Roger ran a sleek and beautifully sharpened Renaissance dagger through the Brexiteer's confusions about the regulatory capabilities of the European Commission, and the UK's existing scope for manoeuvre on this question. Note that in terms of regulatory regime, the EU has no rival in the world bar the United States and the People's Republic. The EU is a regulatory superpower: the only one we have in our part of the western hemisphere and in our time zones. Nevertheless, I repeat; regulatory capability, however vital, is secondary to scale merit.

This means that even if we rushed headlong to develop such regulatory powers, there still would be no sound or sufficiently compelling economic reason for our ever needing them in order to depart from the single market because we would not want to leave; it would not be in our national interest, and so it remains. To argue otherwise is to make a self-defeating mistake, what the philosopher calls 'a category error': a fundamental misreading of economic, political and regulatory

---

[2] The quotation is from a lecture delivered on 23 May 2018 and titled 'The Real Post Brexit Options'.

reality. Or, to put the matter in a more painful contemporary idiom, Adam Smith, Scottish genius and one of the finest minds produced by modern Britain, is the true 'originary' author of everything prudent, cautionary and genuine in the stew of honest anxieties that was at work in what the Brexiteer contemptuously dismisses as 'Project Fear'. Like David Hume, Adam Smith may have been one of the most brilliant Scots who ever lived. Dismiss him, one of the most commanding 'experts' of all time, at your peril.

### AMERICA FEELS CLOSER IN CORK

To arrive in Cork from Wales or the United States is to upset, however slightly, one's sense of transatlantic geography. On the map, cities such as Galway look more or less directly west, across the Atlantic, to the east coast of America. Or so the imagination carries us. But to stand on a beach near Cork, on the south-facing coast, makes one feel that one is on the edge of the Old World; America feels closer in Cork. To travel into the city from the airport is to encounter huge plants bearing proud American names, while the urban landscape is dotted with equally famous US fast-food chains and the like. You expect to find Boston just around the corner.

The capital of Massachusetts is of course the home of that Irish switching yard of the spirit that is Logan Airport. Ernest Renan, the splendid nineteenth-century navigator of the Celtic sensibility, wondered whether a Celt has the ability to spot another Celt no matter how far removed in time and space from the homeland. Renan died before the invention of the airplane, but the Celts of Logan Airport encourage one to entertain this intuitive query by Renan, one of Welsh Brittany's supreme masters of modern thought. More than once I have flown into Logan and been ambushed there when trying to buy a copy of

*The Boston Globe* at an airport shop. The woman on the till spots the accent, and an exchange of tales begins. What county of Ireland? What parochial school? Which orders of nuns, brothers and priests? Before you know it, you are invited home for supper (or more).

All this Irish to-ing and fro-ing between the Republic and America – think of the huge Irish expat communities in New York, San Francisco, Los Angeles and other metropolitan areas – underwrites the Irish appreciation, whether informed or merely instinctual, of one crucial feature of how globalization works. Quite simply, the Irish have got there first, before the English and other Celts, because even before the creation of the single market they had cultivated an intimate, experienced-based understanding of the United States as the continent-sized market model for the European Union. This insight is crucial; but it is one that the Brexiteer who travels frequently to the United States has assiduously sought to ignore.

The contrast between the clear-sighted Irish grasp of American economic reality and the blinkered approach of the Brexiteer pivots, for our purposes here, on this commanding fact: the United States of America is the largest economy within the borders of a single nation in the world because it has, for more than a century and a half, benefited from a single continental-sized free market for labour, a market in which today 325 million people are free to move and work almost anywhere from the Atlantic to the Pacific Ocean.

The free movement of people (and yes, Americans have struggled with all the attendant ramifications, happy and otherwise, that we have experienced here during the past decade) has made the United States the world's pre-eminent economic and military superpower. Only China and the European Union rival it in fact or potential. On its own, the Britain of today and tomorrow never will come close. This is a Celtic statement of a fact – Welsh or Irish, take your pick; either way, it is an objective truth, not a Brexiteer flight of patriotic fantasy. Note further that of the world's three dominant regulatory regimes, only the European Union has offered us a home and a secure place.

POLITICAL BORDERS HARD AND SOFT

To this rational argument for the economic benefits of soft borders, the Irish have added something remarkable: the theory and practice of the soft *political* border. This extraordinary Irish insight draws on the bitter but instructive European experience of two world wars. To put the matter crudely to make a point, these wars were fought over borders. Millions died to defend the supposed sanctity of these once heavily guarded frontiers. Between 1914 and 1945, something between 60 million and 100 million Europeans may have perished in these struggles; but when thoughtful Europeans emerged from the ruins of our continent in 1945, the very idea of rigid national borders no longer carried conviction as a plausible way for organizing Europe and securing its future.

This recoil against carnage on a massive scale ultimately resulted in the transformation of how borders work in Europe – and, more importantly, in the loss of plausibility, by and large, of such symbolically heavily laden frontiers as a reason for going to war. Paradoxically, military specialists, British and others, argue that borderless travel across the EU may be indispensable to the organization of the proper military defence of the European Union's external borders. If our people can move freely, so can our soldiers – and their tanks.

Long in the making, the Schengen Agreement of 1985, which introduced almost unrestricted free movement across the internal national frontiers of participating members of the European Union, embodies both the economic and the political logic of soft

borders. But it is the Irish who have transformed a hopeful aspiration of the thinkers behind what is today the European Union
into reality, because what needed changing was not lines drawn
on a map, but the minds of the people who have cared too much
about drawing lines on maps. One can still find such victims of
the *passé* nineteenth-century obsession with cartography today in
Budapest, Vienna and Chingford. The result of leaving all this
behind in the case of Ireland is the soft border as a philosophy of
mind. Here, a way of looking at geography was transmuted into a
way of being in the world: our world, now.

The results have been astonishing. Breaking with the
nineteenth-century belief in fortified borders, the more rigid the
better, the postmodern enlightened Irish man and woman seeks
to make frontiers as soft and unintrusive as possible. The political
model here would be the plural sense of nationality, as embodied in the Good Friday Agreement, which began to prevail in all
of Ireland after that celebrated Holy Week of April 1998. This
sense of the thing, this political philosophy or metaphysic, has
fallen like soft rain ever since, gradually watering the hard soil
of essentialist nationalism, especially in the North, making the
whole of Ireland that much greener. The famous treaty text, one
of the most consequential in the entire history of international
law, allows an individual, as he or she may choose, to be 'British',
'Irish' or 'Both', in a context where shared membership of the
European Union speaks to a third focus of identity: Europe itself.

I believe that some version of this enlightened practice will
blossom in the other Remain nations after partition. Indeed,
there are ample reasons to believe that this philosophy of mind is
already taking hold. In Cardiff Bay, it is a commonplace assumption. The words 'Welsh' and 'adoptive Welsh' are freely applied,
in a wholly relaxed fashion, to settled residents in the Welsh capital of all colours, creeds and national origins. And this makes
sense in a city that may be one-quarter English – or, better put,

'originally from England' – but then, Cardiff Bay is a confident community with a bustling economy open to all the talents from home and abroad. A tolerant because enlightened Dubliner would be entirely at home among us.

Nevertheless, nowhere in these islands has this plural sense of national identity morphed into a more powerful force for peace and prosperity than in Ireland. The result has been a calming Celtic balm to soothe the troubled spirits of people across the continents whose minds are plagued by doubts and regrets, many of them false and self-harming, about the potential of regionalization and globalization, properly managed and properly regulated, to work, as they must, for us all; because this planet is ours if we can but make it work – together.

The conviction that absolutist ideas of nationalism are at once exhausting and exhausted represents a formidable conceptual breakthrough in how we should think about the foundations of the modern state today. The suggestion would be that a kind of mental barrier has now been breached, certainly in the Remain nations. That is why this bold Irish radicalism of heart and mind, born of unforgiving necessity and considered Celtic realism, has such profound implications for the conduct of international politics, here and everywhere else. And this is also why, as Fintan O'Toole sagely observes, 'the Irish border has such profound implications for Brexit – it is a physical token of a mental frontier that divides not just territories but ideas of what a national identity means in the twenty-first century'.[3]

It is this renewal of our spiritual condition since the horrors of the Second World War that explains our broad feeling of fulfilled contentment with our Remainer marriage of prosperity and diversity. This open stance towards the world holds out the promise of a successful new multinational federal union of self-governing polities: a United Kingdom Federation that is a state worthy of

---

[3] Fintan O'Toole, Ibid.

the name because it has the power and the will to govern, pay and defend. This ambition makes the liberated Irish of the new Ireland our spiritual kin and fellow *ninja* guardians of our infinitely precious treasure of liberal freedoms.

This is why it is so difficult to exaggerate the importance of the contemporary Irish contribution, as fact and as potential, to the deepening social cohesion of the Remain nations. While the angry English nationalist appears to be one of Dante's penitents in hell, head always focused on where he has been rather than where he might go, the Irish invention and animation of the concept and practice of multiple identities stands as our very own Celtic miracle of Lourdes. The instinctual decency and realism at play in the revolutionary opening of the Irish mind to the redeeming virtues of civic tolerance and political pluralism during the past two decades may stand as one of the great turning points in recent global history. Certainly this neglected chapter in the civilizing story of Irish magnanimity and good sense may even now liberate the benighted Brexiteer from the mental chains of his outdated nationalist obsessions.

An optimistic interpretation of Irish history: who would have dreamt of such a thing at the height of the Troubles? Yet it was that vicious, low-grade and seemingly endless struggle between so-called Christian communities in Northern Ireland that helped to spawn our Irish miracle of political pluralism not just as an ideal but as something that millions of human beings believe and practise. The result has been a sigh of moral relief in which even Clio, the paradoxical muse of history, might have rejoiced. The Irish past has been so tormented, so frustrating and so complicated for so long. Now we have a moment to savour, an opportunity to cast a bit of Celtic sunshine on how we tell the story of these islands.

The warmth of this sunshine comforts because, as we shall see, this new caressing temperateness embraces, in fact or potential, all Irish men and women, north and south, without distinction: a hug for us all. This in turn speaks to our Welsh argument, in a chapter on Ireland, because only by a partition, imposed on ourselves, can we help Ireland and Europe, and – if push comes to shove – save our English comrades from the nightmarish dangers posed by the Brexiteer's stealthy conspiracy with the new authoritarians of Putin's Russia and Trump's America.

## Part III - The decolonizing mind: Ireland, Brexit and the Celtic genius

### Rainbow's end

Might this Irish achievement of post-nationalist transcendence, in alliance with an enlightened, secularized Christian sensibility tempered by a globalizing openness and kindness to strangers, qualify as something quietly momentous? Might this Celtic dawn eclipse that Celtic twilight about which Yeats wrote so movingly? Might this Irish experiment in political deconstruction rightly claim a place among those occasional Celtic miracles designed to shelter us from the chaos of invasion and occupation?

Might there, furthermore, be a link of genius between this modern triumph of the spirit and that epoch of Celtic greatness which the Brexiteer would have us forget, that age when an army of literate Irish monks took to the seas and the roads of Europe, armed with books and writing tablets, to strengthen the literate sinews of our civilization in the face of encroaching barbarism as the Roman Empire disintegrated? Just by posing these questions I want to signal that the hour has arrived for us to bury the Irish Question first forged with fire and death by the conquering Tudors, drenched in blood, five centuries ago, by answering it and thereby bringing it to a final definitive close.

This revolution of the spirit, its colour and persuasiveness, registers in the elusive but palpable sense I have that the Irish today have come home – or, in the language of the quest, they have turned their sails homeward – to what they once were, and what they would already be if the English had never come. The old spirits of Celtic life before Rome, before Christianity, before Cromwell, have waited a long time, like souls, for their reanimation in this new chapter in the national life and feeling, most palpable (again that word) in the more modern and confident cities where one finds Ireland's vital centre.

Perhaps inevitably one falls back here on Celtic myth for some sense of the groundswell of delicate, fine-woven sensibility and time-worn anticipation that has begun to grace the new Ireland. This resort to tradition is something at once so premodern and so postmodern that no social scientist, certainly no English social scientist or news commentator (and perhaps that is the point), would dream of indulging. Yet every time I walk the streets of Cork or Dublin today – and this was so even before the Referendum on the Eighth Amendment to the constitution – my mind inevitably returns to the divagation near the end of Proust's famous 'Overture' where he in effect contradicts T. S. Eliot's grim poetic portrait of London filled with the walking dead after the Great War by evoking the Celtic credo that:

> The souls of those whom we have lost are held captive in some inferior being, in an animal, in a plant, in some inanimate object, and thus are effectively lost to us until the day (which to many never comes) when we happen to pass by the tree or to obtain possession of the object which forms their prison. Then they start and tremble, they call us by our name, and as soon as we have recognised their voice the spell is broken. Delivered by us, they have overcome death and return to share our life.[4]

---

[4] From 'Swan's Way', translated by C.K. Scott Moncrieff in 1922.

This intimation about the cycle of life, death and resurrection illuminates. It encourages us to appreciate not only the Welsh passion for forests and the stone emanations of Irish monasticism but also the inspiration behind the great Celtic quests, voyages into the unknown in search of this 'start and tremble', as well as the hopeful impulse at work in the way a mother clings to the prized possession of a dead child as she waits and prays for the child to wake and return. This Celtic belief enriches the subsoil of emotion from which Welsh television dramas as contrasting as *Y Gwyl*, *Requiem* and *Britannia* arise and unfold. It is one of our liberating motifs. It will give us succour and purpose as we emerge from the long ice age of conquest and alien rule. It is why death has not mastered us.

This spirit is at once older than the Sinai of Moses and newer than Yeats's beloved 'death of god' Nietzsche. This spirit alerts us to the sparkling quality of the contemporary transformation of Irish political sensibility. Building on the insights of writers like O'Toole, we might draw on the pacific rigours of the philosopher, and so guided conclude that this ancient spirit is at work still, in the Celtic deconstruction, after Heidegger, Foucault and Derrida, of the essentialist and therefore false ideal of national identity, that most poisonous legacy of the stupid nineteenth century. Granted, this transformation has taken influential shape in Ireland suddenly, during the past two decades or so. But the ground has been prepared since 1922.

There had to be an interregnum of quiet gestation for the spirits of liberty – liberty from Protestant British rule of Catholic Ireland for Protestant British purposes – to blossom, to gain their voice, and thereby to extinguish the spell. Even when most accommodating to the ascendancy, the Church of Rome sheltered the flickering candle of the potential of the Irish to become what they are by giving this hibernating power an indispensable but transitional institutional refuge. This potential was set in ecclesiastical stone, there protected but yearning to live again. Death now overcome, the Celts are ready to share our life with our ancestors of the spirit, both those once dead, now living, and those yet to wake. Today the spell has been shattered. We are nearly free once more.

In the broadest scheme of things, the thinking through of the notion and practice of plural national identities may very well stand as yet another of that series of civilized achievements of the Celtic peoples since St Brendan and other Irish monks of the so-called Dark Ages invented the European sense of space, travel and adventure. This was almost the same era when their Welsh cousins conceived of a humane idea of Nature, proclaimed our comradeship of equality with animals, dreamt the dream of the romantic quest, and celebrated the ideal of civilized relations between men and women. Both of these Celtic projects – the Irish and the Welsh – were united by an unresisting surrender to the seduction and power of story-telling. First do great things, and then celebrate them. Never let the story go untold.

With these primordial innovations, the Celts helped to lay the central foundations of modern European literature and sensibility (Shakespeare, quite frankly, barely compares). Revealingly, this divine gift for creative insight was not exhausted by the epic voyages and inspired fables of our pagan and medieval Christian past. Like that flash of light that illuminates the splendid Caravaggio in the National Gallery in Dublin, the spark of Celtic genius has today struck home in another realm: our newly achieved realization that each one of us may be more than one thing, culturally, ethnically and linguistically. Certainly the mind that gave us Brexit could never have got us to this great, good Irish place of political hope and fluidity just in sight of the steeples of Fermanagh and Tyrone.

# CHAPTER 6

# Making the dream secure: Scottish independence within the United Kingdom Federation

*Human beings are verbs, not nouns. Don't tell me what you are. Tell me what you do.*

## PREAMBLE: SCOTLAND AND THE FEAR OF FLYING

THINKING ABOUT SCOTLAND FROM THE vantage point of Cardiff Bay may simply be a way of misreading Scottish reality, of failing to understand the precise character of the Scottish economy, of mis-appreciating the defining tonalities of the Scottish national sensibility. After all, Wales is a subtle, unobvious place. Why shouldn't the Scots be a subtle and unobvious people as well? Yet sometimes, because the obscuring detail slips out of focus at a distance, the outsider can see the forest for the trees more clearly (and I have the impression, from eavesdropping on the social media debate in Scotland over Brexit, that an interesting number of Scots have a weakness for trees). So what follows is an outsider's view of Scotland, but one informed by undiluted feelings of Celtic solidarity and an unshakeable faith in the Scottish potential for singular achievement and self-mastery. I had a Scottish grandmother (the wife of my Welsh grandfather), so I have some idea what you folk are about.

At first glance, the Scots appear to wear their hearts on the left and their wallets on the right. If the referendum on Scottish independence began with the heart, it was won by the wallet. Curiously, the Scottish vote for remaining in the EU seems to have drawn together both heart and wallet. During the two years after the Brexit vote, the increasingly vitriolic and chaotic war waged by hard-line Brexiteers on the British economy may have done still more to unite the unionist and the nationalist – or should have done, but for those trees.

Faced with the unnerving uncertainties of Tory misrule, one issue looms over all the rest: how is Scotland to pay for independence should the Union falter and partition become inevitable? Can the Scots overcome their apparent fear of flying solo, not at the level of the job market as such but on the home front as a unity? It seems clear to me that Scottish membership of the United Kingdom Federation will provide precisely the kind of reliable economic foundation and safety net that Scottish prudence demands. In this way, the UKF will ensure Scottish dynamism from without.

To enhance Scottish dynamism from within, some of the governing assumptions of conventional Scottish thinking about public policy may have to be recalibrated. With this end in mind, I propose to draw on American insights into the wealth-enhancing powers of what Richard Florida famously called 'the creative class'. Similarly, I propose we tap into the clarity and ambition of American strategies in identifying ways to enhance the average income and net wealth of middle-wage households in Scotland, the very core of the Scottish vital centre.

In all of this, the spirit of the thing is what the nineteenth century called 'muscular Christianity' and the late twentieth century termed 'tough love'. If a Welsh assessment of contemporary Scotland is to leave its mark, the goal must be to engage thoughtfully and sympathetically with fundamental Scottish beliefs about Scotland and its current uncertain place within the United Kingdom; this also requires that we reflect on these beliefs in a hard, clear manner, but always in a friendly spirit. Our goal here is not to belittle Scotland but to help it achieve a new measure of national greatness.

The first part of this chapter therefore aims to press on the Scottish Tory faith not only in old-fashioned unionism but also in the Conservative Party, and then to deconstruct and reconstruct the well-meaning social democratic but increasingly *passé* ideals of some supporters of the Scottish Nationalist Party. Think of this exercise as a good rugby scrap between Scotland and Wales at Murrayfield: no fatalities, just some character-forming bruising. So let us begin with a bruise or two.

## Part I – Partition and the assumption of Scottish unity

> Partition: Division into parts, esp. *Polit.* of a country with separate areas of government.
>
> *The Concise Oxford Dictionary* (1990)

### Is Scotland two nations pretending to be one?

The very notion of partition offends against the ideal of national unity. This may explain why practical examples of partition in the political sense are rare. The raw idea is counterintuitive, almost uncanny. Why would any patriot prefer political division over national unity? For the idea of partition to become persuasive, special circumstances have to apply. In the British tradition, partition has occurred in the recoil against conquest and empire. In this political history, our two prime examples of partition are

Ireland in 1922 and the Raj in 1947. Only the historian can demonstrate whether the Irish example, as policy or just the word, paved the way for the British surrender to the murderous and probably irreversible partition of India and Pakistan into two hostile states.

In retrospect, Jinnah's dream of Pakistan as an Islamic republic was founded on reality: the British Raj at the end was, wisely or unwisely, two states praying apart while pretending to be one, just as the United Kingdom as presently constituted is two states, Leave and Remain, playacting at being one. Such hostility and unrealism mock the definition cited above, which makes partition sound like an administrative convenience: a bloodless mark on a map. Bismarck was closer to the truth when he spoke of 'blood and iron'. The modern state is a brilliant political contrivance of mind floating on the organic, communal, almost visceral foundation of the nation, from the Latin, *natio*, birth.

It is the unravelling of the unity of the English and Welsh nations which is kicking away two of the four legs of the modern British state. In the case of Northern Ireland, sectarian division has always ensured that the Irish leg has been incapable of bearing its fair share of the weight of political responsibility for the effective government of Britain as a whole. This continues to be case. Witness the decisive threat that Northern Irish divisions pose to the UK's chances of negotiating a clean break with the EU.

By contrast, the Irish Republic, freed from this sectarian paralysis, has gone from strength to (fiscal dumping?) strength. The economy of the Republic is now many times larger than that of Northern Ireland. Such statistics should be viewed in the context of the extraordinary resilience the Republic displayed in the face of the brutal aftermath of the Great Recession of 2008–9. As a political system, the United Kingdom lacks any such unity of national purpose, as the referendum vote and its aftermath demonstrate. The Irish Republic is here to stay.

What, then, of Scotland? Uniquely among the four nations of the United Kingdom, only the Scots entertain no notion of a national partition for Scotland because they see no merit in it. They regard themselves as a single nation presided over by a single state. Furthermore, Scottish nationalism tends to be remarkably open to foreigners in general and to Europeans and Europe in particular. The singularly liberal character of the Scottish national credo all but guarantees that the outsider feels barred from speaking to a Scot persuasively about the nature and future of Scotland. Like one of Leibnitz's monads, Scotland is rounded, perfect and coherent. Or so it would appear.

What therefore might the disinterested Welsh realist have to say about the matter of Scotland today? From the vantage point of a Free Wales, Scottish wholeness is best considered politically and then economically, before the two dimensions can be knitted together into a workable but also revolutionary programme. To the Welsh eye, Scotland is politically not so much two nations pretending to be one (I will return to this point in the concluding chapter of this essay to show why this purported unity obscures a major economic flaw) but rather a single state limited by a divided political culture dominated by two contrasting national options – independence or unionism – of which only one is viable: independence.

Romanticism contributes nothing to this realistic Welsh perception. The judgement offered is cold and unfeeling, almost Latin in its logical rigour, and certainly involves no misty nationalistic dreams, however deeply felt, of this or that Celtic utopia. Objectivity is never so forgiving. This is the sobering truth embedded in the metaphor of the British state as a table evoked above: if the Northern Irish leg has always been weak, and the Welsh and English legs are now wobbling vulnerably, it is inconceivable that the Scottish leg can sustain the whole edifice with just this one limb, however sturdy. Tables don't work that way.

## THE UNIONIST ILLUSION

How can we dramatize the fatal blind spot of Scottish unionism? When an American friend of mine, the source of this tale, travelled to London some years ago, he was picked up by his English host at Heathrow and driven to Richmond, where the driver pulled up to a house to park only to reverse and suddenly drive out again in embarrassment. Observing this episode, my American friend smiled and gently asked: 'You mean you don't know where you live?' In a similar vein, it is perfectly predictable that while many Scots wish to preserve the union, this impulse offers no reassuring answer to the question: Union with whom? Thus the root problem of Scottish unionism is that the persuasiveness of the UK union as a political commitment depends on the health of the union beyond Scotland's borders. So where do Scots live? What is Scotland's place today within the national family?

Scottish unionism as an ideal may appear familiar and compelling at home, but unionism does not work, indeed cannot work in any sense, if the union outside Scotland no longer values unionism because the practical worth of the United Kingdom has been exhausted. This is the dagger that the Brexiteer has mindlessly brought to within an inch of the heart of Scottish unionism, and it is not within the power of the Scottish unionist *as a unionist* to deflect the threatening blow. The first cut of this dagger will wound, perhaps fatally, Scottish loyalty to the once deep and straight but now meandering course of the United Kingdom. In the language of Celtic paganism, the old unionism is a dying faith because the British gods have abandoned us.

Were these gods ever faithful to us? Perhaps the current existential crisis of Britishness is bringing to light a fatal flaw in the foundation of the United Kingdom that has been there all along. When in the 1930s the friend of a celebrated American literary wit told her he was going to the proverbially nondescript California city of Oakland, she put on a puzzled expression of disapproval and replied: 'Why? There's no there there'. In the English mind, the Celtic Fringe merits no special attention or interest because, by and large, for them, there is no here here in the Celtic nations. The occasional episode of Scottish pushiness, Irish violence and Welsh whining aside, the Celts barely figure. And we never have. Not really.

The occasional Scottish or Welsh prime minister does not constitute a constitutional principle; such figures offer no definite defence against mindless English majoritarian rough-housing. Note, furthermore, in a point of contrast, that they don't rough-house in Brussels. In Middle England, when the mood takes the fancy of this Brexiteer or that, they use the Welsh flag for target practice. In the capital of the European Union, the Belgians do not take pot shots at the Celts or their flags. So profound doubts arise about the Scottish unionist insistence that two nations (Scotland and Brexit Land) should go on pretending to be one. We are therefore confronted by two interlinked provocations: the sour resentfulness of the Brexiteer as a person with his aggressively impolitic approach to life; and the fate of our constitution, which the Brexiteer has laid low through his innate and uncontrollable fear of change and foreigners.

*Pace* the Scottish unionists' urge to cling to the nurse of unionism for fear of something worse, it is time, perhaps past time, for truth-telling and straight talking about the frayed state of the marriage between Henry Tudor's angry, broken and dysfunctional England and the Remain nations populated by contented, tolerant and able British Europeans. So, as a Welsh marriage counsellor advising the Scots, I have made a judgement that your marriage to the union is dead or dying, and that divorce, as amicable as possible, is the only adult option worth considering. Often accused of being excessively endowed with the proverbial 'gift of the gab', the Welsh nevertheless know how to speak truth to power. So the meditation on your doomed marriage (which is also our doomed marriage) with the union that follows is intended not to rake over the sad, smouldering ashes or to salt wounds, recently inflicted or otherwise, but to do something quite different: my goal is to talk ourselves out of an argument-scarred room via two separate doors marked 'Remain' and 'Leave'.

## PART II – BREXIT TYRANNY AND THE CONSTITUTIONAL DEFENCE OF SCOTTISH INTERESTS

*Is it better to be ruled well by foreigners or badly by one's own?*
A question for an Oxford entrance examination

### BREXIT TYRANNY AND THE BRITISH STATE

The English form the overwhelming majority of the population of our country, and because the UK is what constitutional lawyers and political scientists call a 'unitary state', a majority vote in favour of English interests alone, in a referendum, for example, cannot be legitimately resisted, in the eyes of the majority, by the Celtic minority. Constitutionally, as a minority, we are helpless – not because the constitution provides no safeguards, but because resistance itself is regarded by the political culture as illegitimate: 'You lost,' and that's an end of it.

As in the case of Brexit, we may regard the referendum decision as an existential threat to our national identity and economic well-being, but finally there is nothing we can do as UK dependencies to protect our varied national interests. Certainly we boast few defences against the majority tyranny that the Brexiteer regards as legitimate. Pressed to the wall, Scotland's only option is to submit to the will of the English majority or to escape this form of apparently legitimate democratic tyranny by following the examples of the United States of America and the Irish Republic, and becoming an independent state.

Constitutionally, this is not the whole picture. Tactically, there is a great deal the Celts can do, and are trying to do, to protect our way of life from the economic uncertainties, comedic policy-making chaos and ethnic-cleansing xenophobia of Brexit. The fact that England has two large political parties allows us to play off one against the other. The result of the 2017 general election was so close that even a small Irish political party such as the DUP was able to extract concessions and frustrate the self-serving, invincible ignorance of the Brexiteer on the subject of Ireland. And there is that impressive list of concessions won by Scottish Conservatives from the otherwise distracted May government since the 2017 election. There are also judicial constraints on the exercise of the supremacy of parliament as well as the restraining hand of the House of Lords. Finally, public opinion, too, can help.

Strategically, however, the constitution leaves us naked and exposed to the whims and dreams, fantasies and fears of the English majority. This is the new direct-democracy-rule-by-referendum elephant in the room. Why do we live this way? The simple answer is that all devolved governments in these islands are gifts bestowed by parliament in London on the authorities in Belfast, Cardiff and Edinburgh. It is parliament that does the devolving, and what parliament gives, parliament may take away. This is what direct rule from London means, as any Northern Irish voter can tell you.

From this vulnerable state of constitutional helplessness the spectre of partition arises: if the English ruling class will not govern in our interests, we must do whatever it takes to enable the Scots and the other peoples of the Celtic Fringe to govern ourselves in such a way as to secure the vital interests the Brexiteer so wilfully ignores. Thomas Jefferson, perhaps America's greatest political thinker, would understand our Celtic dilemma, and he would know what to do about it. After all, he drafted his country's Declaration of Independence.

This painful constitutional dilemma is further exacerbated by the perverse spirit of the British constitution: the underlying 'winner-takes-all' psychology of majoritarian bullying that has predictably infected the conduct of the British government since the Brexit vote. Reflecting this political culture, the UK's Brexit majority has shown itself unwilling to conciliate the anti-Brexit minority or take its concerns anything like seriously enough. All this trouble is compounded by the 'first-past-the-post' mentality, the hostility to coalition governments built on compromise, and the parliamentary whipping system that conspires against anti-government views. Thus Tory MPs from Remain constituencies vote to support the government and ignore their Remain voters. Parliament is designed to sustain strong, effective and uncompromising cabinet government at the expense of minority interests because parliamentary minorities as minorities are disqualified from power. The only effective constitutional way a minority can protect itself is to become a majority so that it can bully the old enemy who has lost its own power to bully.

This psychology of majoritarian intimidation has deeply coloured Brexit reportage and commentary in the mass media. The opponent of Brexit is regularly accused of being a 'poor loser', 'a traitor', 'a remoaner' and the like. Tabloid abuse is inflicted on those who legally challenge the Brexit decision and its implementation, the judges who hear such cases and the House of Lords that reviews them. Then there is the astonishing business of the major media figures – individuals such as David Dimbleby, Andrew Marr, Andrew Neil and Piers Morgan – whose interviews with anti-Brexit politicians and citizens and comments on Brexit developments proceed from the dangerous and finally unacceptable assumption that such dissent is intolerable and wrong because the people have spoken and the matter has been settled.

Faced with an aroused, determined, passionate English nationalist majority set on having its way over Brexit, the British system of government has conferred on this majority every tool it requires to work its will and almost none to restrain it. Constitutionally, the elegant result is called 'lump it or leave it'. The Celts as a demographic minority will, in this system, never be safe on their own. Americans drew the same conclusion in 1776 and the Irish rebels did the same in 1922. They wouldn't lump it, so they left.

So, as Lenin asked, 'What is to be done?' Where does all this leave us, strategically and tactically, in the struggle to see off the Brexit tyranny? Our constitutional situation highlights, once again, the overriding importance of the large English minority that voted against Brexit; because all the dangers the Brexiteer will willingly inflict on the Celtic Fringe now also threaten London and the prosperous provincial cities, the homes of the creative classes of Remain England. Why did so many English men and women vote with us?

Part of the answer comes from the new spirit of Irish tolerance, compromise and pluralism that gave us the Good Friday Agreement. This is where the Irish Question, as noted in the previous chapter, becomes the English Question. It is the alchemy of national self-determination and collective *redefinition* that has opened the door for Free Wales and Scotland to join our Celtic brothers and sisters in Northern Ireland to form an alliance with Free England in a new United Kingdom Federation. A new proud era of European freedom now beckons, for all of us – even for the Scottish unionist who is now ready to play a full part in the twenty-first-century destiny of Scotland.

All of this is bracing to a fault. The lessons of the forceful birth of the American and Irish republics hover at the edges of our

fraying national discourse. Certainly the threat of political violence has ceased to be empty pub talk on frosty mornings among
hard lads on Exmoor. The verbal abuse of the Scot who wears the
kilt in Middle England or the Welshman who speaks Welsh on
the wrong side of the border is emblematic of the deeper malaise
behind the random killing of Polish immigrants and the assassi-
nation of the pro-Remain MP Jo Cox. It is such incidents (dismiss
them as aberrations if you dare) that gives the idea of partition its
bite. Speaking of teeth, the Brexit bulldogs must be called off or
else.


CONSERVATISM ISN'T WORKING
In the long and sorry saga of the Brexit negotiations, December
2017 comes close to being the nadir of despairing mirth over the
ability of Westminster as a system to give the United Kingdom
today something approaching proper government. How was it
possible that with all the talent in the British parliament, this
nation's diplomatic fate should end up in the hands of Theresa
May, Boris Johnson and David Davis? In a single week, from 4 to
11 December, the prime minister proposed a set of foggily implau-
sible but supposedly unbending demands, then flew to Brussels
where she jettisoned these red lines in a trice, without explanation, in her negotiations with senior EU officials, only to be called
out of her talks by her junior *faux*-coalition partners, the Brexit
ultras in the DUP. The Northern Irish forced her to abandon
the negotiations and fly home in an act of personal and national
humiliation.

At which point the whole dance began again with another set
of proposals hammered out by Number Ten in frantic overnight
talks with all and sundry, followed by a dawn return flight on
Thursday to Brussels for the prime minister, resulting in a fresh
agreement with the EU opening up the possibility of trade talks

in the New Year. After all this, one would have hoped that this English bedroom farce dressed up as high policy-making had reached some form of sensible conclusion; but no, David Davis, the Brexit Secretary, spurred on by a senior but anonymous leaker in Number Ten, declared that Britain was not bound by Mrs May's agreement with Brussels and Dublin because it was 'meaningless'.

Such examples of almost comic misrule offer the most important demonstration of why the Brexiteer's approach to economic reality and policy-making will never work in practice, because no government, of whatever ideological colour, can function in this way. The prime motive behind the urge to create a United Kingdom Federation is to shield us from such forms of chaotic misrule. This is why, in the first instance, the three Celtic Remain nations look to Free England to join in a common defence against such systematic forms of political incompetence. To invest such hopes in a heroic mission for a Free England is a final grand and prayerful Celtic gesture of loyalty to the former greatness of the old United Kingdom. It is the most practical option for the Remain nations within an otherwise dying and dysfunctional system of unionism.

Let us examine more closely one of Theresa May's major pronouncements on Brexit, her Lancaster House speech of 17 January 2017, nearly seven months after the referendum vote. This speech by the prime minister is officially the most important of these interventions because it was viewed, certainly at the time, as a statement of government policy, and as her most serious bow to hard-Brexit orthodoxy. In retrospect, it is obvious the Lancaster House address did not reflect government policy because there isn't one: the Tory government and party are utterly divided over Brexit. Indeed, Mrs May's speech was not even a summary of cabinet policy, because no serious player in the cabinet appears willing to submit to a shared policy line or negotiating strategy. Finally, it is not even obvious the Lancaster House speech reflects the prime minister's personal view of the matter, given the disingenuous and often contradictory language in which supposedly inviolable policy 'red lines' are set forth.

What else is one to make of the humiliating retreats, instant and comprehensive, inflicted by Brussels on London after the negotiations with Michel Barnier began in the summer of 2017? Or the sudden burst of 'Zulu dawn' bolshiness by the prime minister after she was ambushed by the (not very) European Research Group led by Jacob Rees-Mogg in 2018? Every other month during the autumn and winter of 2017 yet another Brexit non-negotiable demand succumbed, only to be resurrected some months later like the undying villain in a Hollywood horror film.

It is easy to dismiss this Tory collapse into pretence, incoherence and obscurantism as High Tory piffle until one realizes that this closing of the Brexit mind is a direct consequence of the baleful impact of a debased form of English metaphysics. This defect of mind may pose by far the most insidious danger to the future of the UK, no matter what the outcome of the Brexit struggle, because it will persist uncured. In defeat or victory, this English patient will not get better. This mental disability verges on the genetic; it's in the Tory DNA.

Since the referendum vote of 1975 to join the European Union, the vital link between thought and speech, reality and the perception of reality has been fatefully broken in the Brexiteer's brain. For the Welsh realist, the worst blow was the revelation that grand Tory pledges mean nothing. A policy promise announced by Downing Street on Monday is completely reversed on Wednesday only to be kicked into touch on Friday. Then it becomes a red line over the weekend and this brings us back to a blank sheet (or cheque) on Monday, when the same dance begins all over again. This is not government. It is certainly not a system or mode of government in which the minority Celtic vassal nations of the United Kingdom can prudently invest their faith. So where's the British 'there' in all of this? Where is this unionist union to which we should be committed and faithful for so little compensation in return? As a Welsh realist I would prefer my country to be a valued dependency of Europe rather than a passenger held hostage on this driverless bus of Tory misrule verging on chaos. Wouldn't you?

So what does the Lancaster House speech reflect? From the point of view of the Celtic Fringe and the four Remain nations, Mrs May's address appears to have been a tortured exercise in word magic designed to hold the Tory Party together and keep the prime minister in Number Ten. For the Remain voter, there were some honeyed words and kind slogans. For the Celtic nations, however, Mrs May's stance was emphatic: no matter how profound the existential threat posed by Brexit, especially in the form of a hard Brexit or 'no deal', to our security, our prosperity, our identity and our future, we are constitutionally exposed to any majoritarian chill that blows in from the Brexit heartland. One quote from the Lancaster House speech, slightly recast, drives home this larger point:

> There are two ways of dealing with different interests. You can respond by trying to hold things together by force, tightening a vice-like grip that ends up crushing into tiny bits the very things you want to protect. Or you can respect difference, cherish it even, and reform the EU so that it deals better with the wonderful diversity of its member states.

Just alter 'EU' to 'UK', and the plight of the Celtic Fringe under threat from Brexit tyranny becomes vivid and intolerable. Making the rounds of Celtic governments in Belfast, Cardiff and Edinburgh, Mrs May made her policy stance *vis-à-vis* Northern Ireland, Wales and Scotland punishingly clear. For the cameras, she went through a choreographed pretence of listening to our leaders. Behind closed doors, she then ignored those leaders by loftily dismissing our hard-won right to protect our national interests. In Scotland, the unionists either conspired with this imperious disregard or played the paper tiger.

Constitutionally, May has hung the Celts out to dry. Ironically, only the anti-EU DUP in Ulster has managed to trip up the Brexit Tory as if by accident, but the incidental twists and turns of coalitions there have only emphasized the inherent weaknesses of the British constitution. This dispiriting marriage of contemptuous indifference to the Celtic Fringe and shambolic misrule from No. 10 Downing Street embodies a drastic failure of national governance. Such calamities do not happen in Brussels because the Council of Ministers and the Commission know where Dublin and Athens, to cite two pertinent examples, are on a map and why they matter. Commission hardball, however bruising and tough, is at least a game played by two sides; dismissal by constitutional fiat is not a proper political game of any kind, and is certainly not one that the Celtic nations will ever find is worth playing. So the correct answer to our Oxford examination question is obvious: QED (again).

## PART III – THE CREATIVE CLASS: AN INTRODUCTION FOR SCOTTISH BREXITEERS

*Fifty per cent of all employees in California's Silicon Valley are not Americans.*

BREXIT AND THE TRIUMPH OF THE CREATIVE ECONOMY
Just over a century ago, Max Weber published *The Protestant Ethic and the Spirit of Capitalism*. Weber was one of the founding fathers of the modern social sciences; this beloved German thinker is the man who helped ensure that ideas such as 'charisma' and the 'work

ethic' even now occupy an influential place in how we discuss contemporary politics, society and the economy. For our purposes here, Weber was a seminal critic of both Adam Smith and Karl Marx because he emphasized the importance of non-economic values (religious and otherwise) to the triumph of modern capitalism in the West.

A century on, Richard Florida and his colleagues in a dozen fields of research have seized on a set of values that are not strictly economic but, in a manner similar to Weber's argument, have transformed the global economy. Florida would have us brood carefully on three interrelated ideas: the human compulsion to be creative (inside and outside the workplace); the creative social class as the embodiment of a set of values by which it is defined; and the creative economy as a whole viewed as a human enterprise that transcends the cash register and the imperatives of the accountant while – and here is a lovely paradox – effectively improving society's bottom line.

So where do we find the creative sectors whose importance has been so marginalized in the Brexiteer's war on real existing capitalism? Searching for definitions of the creative economy, one Scottish government website notes that, 'in the UK, the sector is generally regarded as being made up of 13 distinct industries – advertising, architecture, art and antiques, crafts, design, designer fashion, film, interactive leisure software, music, performing arts, publishing, software and computer services and TV and radio'. This definition strikes me as crabbed and uninspiring. It fails to capture or reflect the joyous energy of the creative industries. The thinking behind this overview seems to hark back to old-fashioned top-down philosophies of public policy-making – but it is a start.

It is encouraging that Scottish unionists display a keen awareness of the significance of the creative class for our future which is rarely matched south of the border. Indeed, few Tory think-pieces on this strategic challenge, whether on the ConservativeHome website or elsewhere, exhibit more than the slightest recognition that the creative economy is a creation of creative individuals and communities that must be understood for what they are, and on their terms.

Once the politician, corporate leader and public-policy intellectual learn to stoop and not conquer, we may begin to reflect sensibly on how large organizations, beginning with the state, might help the creative classes – or, more to the point, how the conservative nationalist might hinder them. In short, the concerns that dominate the minds of the Brexiteer – immigration, national sovereignty and blue passports – do not speak to the imperatives of the creative classes because our passions are so fully engaged elsewhere. Observe how the creative *joie de vivre* of the engaged creative is almost entirely absence from Brexit Land. Fun is one thing that the Brexiteer isn't. The United Kingdom Federation is another country.

So now, in our UK endangered by the uncertainties of Brexit, it is imperative that we narrow the disturbing gap that still persists between official elite thinking (on both right and left) and the mental world of the creative class. By looking at the urban nodes of the creative economy we can put some flesh on what are often rather bloodless (and therefore misleading) official descriptions. For me, the formidable exponent of this new vision may Richard Florida, the influential American architect and urbanist. At the beginning at the current century, he proclaimed the arrival of new class in modern society: the creatives. He thought it included perhaps a third or so of the workforce, and ranged over all the artforms, traditional and modern, as well as engineering and the sciences, indeed all and everyone whose job is mainly a creative endeavor.

In the context of any analysis of the cultural divide between Leavers and Remainers, Florida insistence on the liberal openness that characterizes the creative classes is particularly salient. The unshakable commitment of the creative man and woman to what I call the 'four 't's' (tolerance, tempered technology and talent') offers no quarter to the advocate of ethnic cleansing, white hegemony or illiberal reaction. To put the matter bluntly, to seek 'to take back control' of our borders is to make war on the most dynamic, most profitable and most rapidly growing sectors of the national, European and global economy. In this sense, Brexit represents the rejection of our future as a creative civilization. So which side of this argument is the Scottish unionist on? Are you for the free movement of people or not?

WHERE DOES THE CREATIVE CLASS WANT TO LIVE?

Guided by the strict assumption that creativity requires diversity, where does Florida locate the most impressive nodes of creative class growth and success? In searching for the answer, Florida argued, it was essential to look beyond America's recognized centres of talent clusters and start-up frontiers (Manhattan, Miami, Los Angeles, San Francisco and Seattle, for example), and pay closer attention to the subtle interplay of bohemian liberal values, female and gay 'creatives' and ethnic cosmopolitanism so vigorously on display in the exceptional centres of value creation that Florida and his colleagues first discovered in places such as Boston, Austin and Nashville.

To read Florida in a nuanced way is to appreciate why Cardiff, with its vibrant music scene, its large student population, and its self-selecting, self-generating and self-sustaining 'people culture' offers a British example of the metaphoric womb of amniotic fluid in which the vital centre can take shape and where the creative class can find a home. It is against this Welsh example that one understands why Florida found that even enlightened Pittsburgh's top-down efforts to attract and retain the cream of the creative classes produced by its splendid universities (including Florida's own Carnegie-Mellon) tended to lose out to more dynamic places such as Boston and Austin. He found that creative young people wanted to work where other creative people worked.

The resulting communities were open, diverse, tolerant and often fantastically successful. Indeed, the arrayed forces of an army of creative individuals have proven so profitable that many firms have had to learn to chase these creatives, thereby breaking with the classic assumption that individuals must always pursue the firm. This imperative has been fuelled by a striking alliance of liberal values and bottom-line realism. Note that the stereotypical Tory reactionary is tone deaf to the new mood music of enlightened progress.

For the Brexiteer, the implied warning is grim: make these creative people seriously uncomfortable in any way, and they will abandon the UK for somewhere more sympathetic to their creative needs and values. Unconstrained freedom of movement speaks to these needs and values. This is why creatives find the European Union so congenial. This in turn explains why partition may offer us the best means of heading off the potentially massive brain drain that the Brexiteer would inflict on us. So, again, the question must be posed: is the Scottish unionist for or against this potential haemorrhage of precious talent from many of Scotland's most profitable because most creative industries and sectors? If the Tory Party is to play a practical role in the UKF tomorrow, one-nation Scottish Tories must prepare to split from the Tory right if a creative future for Scotland is to be defended.

Today, Florida's seminal argument must be pushed forward and its relevance to our contemporary situation asserted even more strongly because of the political crisis in which we now find ourselves. To this end, I offer here some reflections on the indispensable contribution that the creative classes will make to the cause of Scottish economic self-mastery (and indeed the economic self-mastery of us all), hung on five points. First, we must master the implications of the insights generated by nearly two decades of research and debate over the role of the creative classes, and then fold them (like whipped cream) into our assessment of Brexit. Second, we need to elaborate in more detail why the creative classes (when they are politically aware) are overwhelmingly pro-Remain. Third, we must clarify the ways in which the Brexiteer threatens the overriding commitment of the creative classes to 'tolerance, tempered technology and talent'. Fourth, we must attempt to elaborate the life-cycle of the creative classes (something hitherto relatively neglected by writers on the creative economy). And five, we must propose effective ways for the creative classes to safeguard ourselves from the Luddite ravages of the neo-nationalist authoritarians who support Trump, Putin and Brexit.

### The individual talent: genius on the street where I live

One of the best things that can happen to a young Scottish child with creative potential is to turn a page or look through a window and be confronted with the high-backed elegance and craft of a Mackintosh chair. Beyond all the other ingredients that make a Scottish child a Scot, such encounters are gloriously enriching because these chairs demonstrate that creativity on a singularly high level is possible on the street, as it were, where that child lives, in the community, large or small, that this son or daughter of Scotland calls 'home'. Let us use this example of the Mackintosh chair as a vantage point from which to view the indispensable core of Scotland's vital centre: the Scottish creative classes.

In some ways I envy the Scottish child ambushed and entranced by a 'Hill House 1' design. There was no native American equivalent of a Scottish Mackintosh chair that spoke to me as a child in the respectable working-class community where I grew up in Los Angeles. The great city itself could boast a world-dominating film and television industry, but these wonders left my psyche yearning for a different kind of creative perfection, and this I found (or did it find me?) in the Japanese aesthetic that coloured almost every aspect of the lives and spaces of the Japanese-American community that surrounded me as a young schoolboy. In this way, a creative quest was born; the resulting need, for the imagined dwelling of creative perfection, took me thousands of miles from Los Angeles to Japan. In this way, the modest understated Oriental gardens of Gardena, a childhood enriched by immaculately wrapped paper-covered *ko-mono*, the beguilement of the mysterious *Kanji* calligraphy on the walls of local shops, and the uncanny meditative calm that still governed these Japanese homes in exile made me a peripatetic; not a wanderer but a young man with a quest.

In this way, the creative individual puts unyielding corrective pressure on the idle assumption that 'somewhere people' are superior to 'anywhere people', because so many talented creatives are not 'somewhere people' rooted in the soil of the past or locked in a dull prison of hidebound domesticity. Quite the contrary, they very quickly learn that to breathe and flourish creatively, they must seek out places that feed and foster their creative urges. This need trumps all other imperatives, including the claims of home and hearth. In short, if the community of one's birth and childhood cannot nurture this creative need, one leaves. If your nation chooses to make war on you as a creative person, you will abandon it. Here is Brexit as brain drain.

Conventional Scottish nationalism, like all nationalisms everywhere, is mute on this point. It has nothing to say about the central issue at hand here, because creativity and the need to be creative trump familism, localism, the tribe, the 'hood' and ethnic identities of all kinds. The insight in question is strict in what its most values: it was not Scottish nationalism that made Mackintosh great, but Charles Rennie Mackintosh who put his country on the map of design greatness. He comes first. He is primary. Genius always is.

If Mackintosh and his creative peers had been absent from the Scottish scene, even more creative Scots would have set sail in search of aesthetic Shangri-Las outside Scotland: Paris, Italy and beyond. Recall all the creative shuffling between Pittsburgh and Austin that Florida and his colleagues discovered took place within the borders of a single vast nation; or, more importantly still for our purposes here in Europe, consider all this creative motion unfolded within a single vast economic market for talent.

For the creative person, that is what the single market of the European Union is: a continental-sized creative laboratory, and a thrilling one at that. To see the workings of the creative spirit from this standpoint is to begin to fathom why European creatives, including those among the Celts and the English, tend to value the all but frictionless travel to the continent that the European Union has fostered. For the European creative, the EU platform is a launch pad and diving board from which to leap into encounters with the wide world of creative ideas being pursued outside Europe; but it is the single market for creative talent that makes us players in this global *atelier*.

No paradox is involved here. Because of the creative power of their cultures, Japan and the United States figure prominently in the decorator products and design ideas our company sources from abroad. Nevertheless, for us and our company, now expanding from Wales to Bordeaux and Sicily under the lash of the Brexiteer, it is France and Italy that form the core of the geographic heartland of classic architecture and design innovation. With these provinces of aesthetic genius, we share an unresisting because organic relationship. What Heidegger and St John Paul II called the 'House of Europe' is our gloriously creative home. The creative sinews of this superpower of the artistic, scientific and technological imagination stretch from Stockholm to Palermo, from Tallinn to Porto.

Let us conclude this brief meditation on the geography of creative originality by returning to the Scottish child contemplating a Mackintosh chair for the first time. That instant may be, for that child as a creative being, the supreme moment of self-revelation. The entire trajectory of that child's career and creative life will henceforth be governed by a single imperative: 'Because Mackintosh succeeded, I must try.' Thus is established an enduring mental frontier between the 'before' of creative sleep and the 'after' of creative exhilaration: *Creamus, ergo sumus.*

## THE PSYCHOLOGY OF CREATIVITY AND SCOTTISH POLITICS

In all their variety, the creative classes who animate our creative industries are united by a single overarching principle. As a member of the creative class, my job is to make or conceive of something new, and my creative input into my enterprise (however defined), whether I am a solitary writer in a garret or a genius CEO, is what determines my place, my contribution, my material compensation and my satisfaction in what I do. It is my reason for living, as a professional and as an artist, in the universal sense. The continuous and therefore ever renewing need to conceive and shape, to listen and understand, is what makes the creative person what he or she is. In the words of Ilse Crawford, the influential English interior designer and product innovator (for clients including Ikea, for example), creation is 'a thought process' and 'a skill' that unites the craft of 'interrogation' with a gift for 'empathy' that aims to enhance the lives of all.

Taken together, these elements form an impressive creative palate and set of talents to be cultivated. They all feed what Bergson called our *élan vital*: this hunger, this drive, this compulsion. For the creative person, the imperative of a life well lived is creativity or nothing. And it cannot be 'nothing'. This relentless insistence on achieving creative fulfilment in one's life as a human being – how else is one to ensure that one's talent achieves its fullest flowering? – is what puts the creative classes among the dominant economic drivers of the global marketplace today, in Scotland and everywhere else. This class of people transcends almost all national, cultural, religious and ethnic barriers, because when you encounter another person who shares your creative passion, all the other things that might divide you from that person become secondary. The colour of her passport is entirely irrelevant to her as a factor in her identity as creative person. For us, a blue passport is not a soul.

In place of these barriers, and the static and undeconstructed identities they reflect (borders, flags, races and religions), the creative classes exhibit a principled embrace of our 'Three (or Four) Ts'. Richard Florida's triplet of talent, tolerance and tempered technology might stand as shorthand for a holy trinity of almost divine secular values. These values do not constitute a surrender to the liberal niceties of political correctness; they are, in Florida's own words, 'an economic necessity'. There is no commercial alternative that works anything like as well. Taking the idea of 'design' in its broad sense, Ilse Crawford speaks for all creatives, here and abroad, when she insists that our labours must 'enhance our humanity' by making the world, and the space where we live our lives in the world, better, more human, happier and more fulfilled.

Florida's theory appears, nearly two decades on, to be scientifically robust (despite even his doubts). His propositions or academic theories have been repeatedly put to empirical test by statisticians and scholars. Unlike the untested and unempirical claims of the Brexiteer ideologue, the assertion that the creative class as a whole is the most economically successful component of the post-Fordist economy can be advanced with confidence; it is the component that is growing fastest in relation to other sectors of the economy. For millions of people around the globe, the creative economy has been quite simply more successful in securing robust job security for its practitioners through all the vicissitudes of the business cycle, at least since the 1990s, than any of its rivals.

In Scotland, the importance of the creative classes is often given public recognition and support of a kind not always matched elsewhere in the United Kingdom. The Scots, in this sense, point the way forward; they are not half-hearted in their endorsement of and commitment to the UK's creative class. Via their public remarks on the importance of Scotland's creative industries, the two women who, when viewed from Cardiff Bay, appear to dominate Scottish politics – Nicola Sturgeon and Ruth Davidson – position us to see an important truth: the key to a successful Scottish future turns on the almost dialectical interaction between the solutions that the Remainer creative offers for the failures of the Scottish Leave community who so bitterly feel left behind. So, to put the matter concisely, the cure for those who have been overtaken by the rapid pace of globalization is to become creative and join the successful creative classes, or marry a creative, or spawn a creative or two in the next generation among their own offspring. Politically, the aspirational working class should extend its hand to form an alliance with us to resist the encroaching dangers of reactionary darkness and discord.

This formula is premised on the assumption that every human being has some gift for creativity. The left behind can make a contribution – indeed, he or she must make a contribution, because the future of the planet is best served by everyone making their creative contribution to our collective well-being. There is no reason and no excuse to waste the most important resource of all: human creativity. And this brings us to a still sterner truth: we creatives will not carry those who feel economically left behind, indeed, we cannot not carry them, if they insist on making war on us as a creative class. Anyone who voted for Brexit and continues to support Brexit, with all the damning and unnecessary economic damage that entails, is making war on us. This, too, will not do.

The logic of the creative class and its cluster of values have been all but completely ignored by the Brexiteer voter, Jeremy Corbyn, UKIP and the right wing of the Conservative Party. Many of these people remain prisoners of economic doctrines and political dogmas that had already lost their relevance and explanatory power with the post-war transformation of the globe after 1945. As a result, these politicians have lost touch with the practical needs of individuals and families today, whatever their level of education, their net worth and their aspirations for the future.

Granted, the 'alt-right' billionaire ideologue does have an unappetizing (chlorinated-chicken) vision of the future, and given his relentless hunger for the power that proceeds from ever fatter untaxed wallets, he may temporarily triumph over the rest of us – as may the dark satanic mills of the web boiler room. In the end, however, even if it takes another Eighty Years War of resistance such as that fought by the Dutch, we will vanquish the greedy Brexiteer because, like the Nazis who conquered Europe, his dystopian nightmare of the future has nothing finally to offer any of us. Why? Because his maddened ideas are threadbare of humanity and hope – and creativity.

## PART IV – PAYING FOR FREEDOM: WEALTH-CREATION STRATEGIES FOR THE AVERAGE SCOTTISH FAMILY AFTER INDEPENDENCE

### 'GHOST BREXIT' AND THE BIG PICTURE

Part of the reason why nationalist visions for our country appears to be so spiritually and intellectually thin may be found in what I call 'ghost Brexit': the large technological, economic and demographic changes that may transform how we live but are rarely factored into our intense argument over Brexit. Think of the challenge to the world of work posed by automation and robotics. Developments such as this will transform the meaning of being 'left behind' economically because millions of jobs are under threat, and not only at the low-skill service end of the economy.

Take another item that figures only slightly on the Brexit agenda: the unsettling impact of crypto-currencies, such as Bitcoin and the like. Bitcoin mining is a curious phenomenon, a highly energy-dependent industry apparently created by an anonymous algorithmic investor. Leaving aside these odd spin-off activities, crypto-currencies as speculative ventures are often viewed as a predictable response to the steady debasement of national and regional currencies by governments and central banks. The short-term opportunities for windfall profits they offer address the hunger for convenient ways to contain the rise of household debt. They also reflect discontent with the arbitrary corporate regulation and restriction of conventional financial institutions, such as banks, online payment companies and the like.

More revealing still is the right-wing neglect of demographic change. British critics of the European Union make much of the relative decline of the EU's economy *vis-à-vis* emerging economies elsewhere, but the relative demographic decline of the white population poses a much more severe challenge to the ethnic nationalist and any proponent of identity politics. There is much talk of the political, economic and social consequences of non-white immigration, legal or otherwise, but relative silence on the absolute decline of white numbers resulting from our declining reproduction rates. How many families do you know that have at least three children, the bare minimum required for demographic survival?

Here there occurs an unlikely overlap between the abortion debate and globalization, particularly with the Evangelical embrace of scripture's call to 'increase and multiply', but this also tends to be a ghost argument for the Brexiteer. Finally, there are the massive fiscal implications of the social and medical care required by our greying population. Who is going to pay for the NHS if we send our creative classes into exile? The Brexiteer economist does not have an answer.

Nevertheless, this ghost debate should focus our concerns on the underlying pull and tug affecting the creative who is married to his vocation and on the future decline of employment across a range of occupations. Ideas of a universal income are one response. Increasing the number of people who can live without work because of their investment income is another. Everywhere in these discussions the pressing national need for enhanced economic literacy and the business of economic self-mastery loom large. So the question that matters is: how do we want to live our lives? What kind of human beings do we want to be? How do we want to spend the finite number of days granted to us on this earth? The colour of our passports does not begin to address these questions. And so we arrive at the beaches of southern California.

CALIFORNIA DREAMIN': AN INCOME-DOUBLING PLAN FOR SCOTLAND
If Scots were twice as rich as they are – if everybody across the board had twice the income and twice the net wealth they have at present – would they vote for independence? I suspect that the voter from the heart would exclaim 'Yes!' while the wallet faction would enthusiastically assent but only if this doubling of income and net wealth were sustainable: not a one-time lucky lottery win, but a system for a dynamic and growing new Scotland. The income-doubling plan I am proposing will address the concerns of both the Scottish heart and the Scottish wallet. But to understand what I have in mind, we need to make a journey of the imagination to a very different place: post-war southern California.

When the Welsh side of my family migrated to the United States from Pontypridd, just north of Cardiff, they ended up in Colorado, in a gold-mining community high in the Rocky Mountains. At an elevation of three thousand metres (just under ten thousand feet), mining had achieved the unlikely miracle of bringing slag heaps to the Himalayas. The high Rockies took their revenge on me, a child born at sea level, whenever I was tempted to dash out of the old family home to play on those slag heaps only nearly to pass out because the air was so thin.

These Welsh migrants brought more than the detritus of mining to Colorado. They also imposed the easy solidarity of the proverbial Welsh mining community on the anarchic craziness of a gold-rush throng after its first mad flush. Such mining communities produced more than gold; they produced enduring social bonds. When the price of gold collapsed in the 1930s and a building boom (accelerated by the Second World War) transformed California, my parents moved to Los Angeles, and there, yet again, recreated a kind of Celtic network of former Coloradans (mainly Welsh, with a leaven of Irish and Scots) in the suburbs of what was then America's third largest city.

Perhaps inevitably, if you know anything about Welsh towns and villages, this form of solidarity ensured that among our extended network of friends and relations in southern California, the urban refugees from the Rockies were the ones who counted socially (only my friends from my parochial school days mattered as much to me, someone, to be fair, who has never been allowed to work down a mine).

There are two larger points at issue here. The majority of these economic migrants in search of a better life, first in Colorado and then California, benefited enormously from southern California's long post-war property boom. Wherever my family, as part of this Colorado diaspora, metaphorically moored their boats, property values enhanced their net worth by lifting these boats. When retirement approached, decent pensions made up for lost salary income but, more important, mortgage-free property miraculously enhanced household net worth in the form of a pool of capital sufficiently large to buy a down-sized retirement home and leave a residue to reinvest the assets that could generate income streams; rental properties, for example.

Such investments, in property or stocks and shares, proved a god-send when, in later life, medical bills mounted and nursing-home costs had to be paid. Even here, though, the sums generated by property sales and the like, while not enormous, often allowed my parents' generation to leave generous legacies for mine. With a minimum of prudence and skill, my generation will be able to do the same. Note that no great knowledge or financial sophistication were involved in this exercise of net worth doubling (or more). Besides the honed discipline of the Protestant work ethic (my father's family were Welsh-speaking Baptists), only one virtue mattered throughout this saga: the willingness to move home in search of a superior material standard of life.

Family history inculcated the sober, semi-conscious awareness that the economic fortunes of oneself, one's family and one's community were determined by the tidal flows of global economic forces. When these tidal flows were friendly, one exploited them to the full. When they turned contrary, the individual, the family and the community took to the seas and highways in search of a better life. The confident assumption, proven by experience, was that if globalization caused our woes, globalization could provide the cure. Somewhere salvation would be found. In my family and my community, so described, very few were ever tempted to sing the old musical ditty, and now the new Brexiteer anthem: 'Stop the world, I want to get off'.

This success story, this triumph of family and community over economic ill-fortune, makes a complete mockery of the supposed superiority of 'somewhere people' over 'anywhere people'. I am not tempted to spend time with my relations in Pontypridd or Wrexham because almost immediately after one sat down to tea, a furious argument would threaten over the economic fate of those who left versus those in stayed, and I can tell these folk will not cheerfully bear the bruising thwack of a 'Welsh boomerang' (which, in immigration terms, is what I am because of the Welsh belief in blood ties). This argument is, of course, a fight that the Welsh diaspora cannot lose. Talented or untalented, educated or uneducated, nearly everyone who left south Wales for southern California ended up richer than those who stayed. There were and are exceptions – but not enough to challenge the wisdom of paying attention to trends in the global economy, something by and large the stay-at-homers refuse to do on principle (in the spirit of Catherine Tate's unlovable 'Lauren', they can't be bothered).

Why does this argument that sets 'somewhere people' versus 'anywhere people' matter to Scotland today? Two reasons figure larger than the rest. First, the Scottish decision to resist the pattern that will prevail in the other three nations of the United Kingdom and decline to embrace national partition means that the often economic moribund 'stay-at-homers' will be kept (in both senses) within the national fold: wealthier Scots will be expected to pay for the indigents who either cannot or will not pay their own way.

Second, implicit in the Scottish nationalist model is the assumption that the Scottish economy by itself can cope with every ripple and wave of the ever-fluctuating currents of the global economy. Whatever its attractions as a political model and ideal, the unitary state does not embody economic wisdom in the age of globalization. President Trump's promise to recover the jobs that the industrial Midwest has lost may succeed. Some jobs may be brought home. But then no one will leave Pennsylvania, Michigan or West Virginia; too many will stay put, and therefore no one will ever learn about the need to move. This will guarantee their helplessness in the face of global economic change. The same logic applies with the same relentless force to the fate of the denizens of Neath, Grimsby or Teesside.

This is the stuff and substance of defeat. Just as the coal boom of the late nineteenth century lifted the fortunes of my Welsh ancestors, so the death of King Coal let them fall. Just as the Colorado gold rush resurrected their fortunes amid the slag heaps in the Rockies, FDR's decision to abandon the gold standard threatened their jobs in the mines. Just as the property market of California redeemed their fortunes after the Second World War, some new nemesis may be lying in wait around a future corner. True, we could have stayed at home in the Welsh valleys and survived; but we would not have flourished as working-class people on anything like the scale we achieved in California. And neither will Scots who ball-and-chain themselves to 'somewhere'.

This perception underwrites the implicit wisdom of Scotland's determination to remain in the European Union, as a population of just over five million in an economic market of half a billion people. The single market is larger than Scotland by a factor of a hundred. The multiplication table of potential family fortunes implied is irresistible in the face of the economic uncertainties of tomorrow. From this perspective, any Scot who voted to leave the single market in the name of national sovereignty or fish quotas or migrant controls has simply no grip whatever on the economic realities of the world as it is. These people have not lost their minds, but they have lost their way, and therefore they are on the way to losing their wallets. Are you ready, now you have a bruise or two, for something you can rarely get in southern California: a proper cup of tea?

## WHY ARE THE RICH RICH?

Among this Los Angeles diaspora, there were a handful of families who invested wisely not only in their homes, where they lived, but in rental properties, in order to buy and rent still more properties.

Buying and 'flipping' houses or apartments figured in this strategy but mainly as a part of the search for better rentals. With this mode of income expansion and property empire-building, albeit in a minor key, the most ambitious of the Colorado diaspora crossed the invisible frontier that divides owning (mainly) liabilities from owning (mainly) assets. The distinction is crucial, for a liability, in my sense, is something that we must pay for while an asset is something which pays us: in this example, the rental and sale income from land and buildings.

By such capitalist alchemy, these investments transmuted into a sustained income stream via rents and dividends – an income stream that demanded little or no work. The accountant's quarrel over how many angels can fit on the roof of an asset is finally not the point. Rather, the key phrase here is 'income stream'. These income streams do not depend on salaries. Therefore you can retire or become seriously ill and still have an income from your property as long as the property is a genuine asset (you don't live in it and the mortgage does not bankrupt you). Most people in the Western world, including Scotland, have few assets and many liabilities (an issue to which we will return). Among the most financially successful, because prudent, of the Colorado diaspora, investment in property was just one of the ways these ambitious people paved the way towards financial independence, in some cases well before retirement age. More interestingly, from the standpoint of our concern with doubling average household incomes in Scotland, some of these prudent families became millionaires. In this way, we arrive at the first and much the largest of three key numbers or numerical indicators that are germane to this argument: a million pounds in net wealth.

Now, a million pounds is a very interesting number, because that is the sum that is required to generate an annual investment income, more or less risk-free, approaching £50,000 (the second of our three indicators), be it from stocks and shares or rental properties or some other income-stream-generating investments.

Outside London and the most expensive districts of Scotland's wealthiest cities, a family with £50,000 of unearned income will lead a very comfortable life without employment: a high standard of living, plus scope for expensive travel, charity giving and post-retirement projects that may be economic liabilities but that are not only fun but affordable. More interesting still, households that live on income streams of £50,000 appear to be, in many modern economies, the most contented of all income brackets. To have less than £50,000 is to strain a bit; to have more is to tempt the gene of avarice – or so the social statisticians tell us.

These figures give us a goal for doubling average household income in Scotland. Note, for example, that with such an income it becomes possible for the household to pay for child-minders, social care or private medical insurance (or cash on the day for private medical care). It might also be possible for people in this income bracket to renounce the state pension as an act of civic virtue. Note that in this tour of Scotland's financial horizon we have distanced ourselves, as the backbone of Scotland's vital centre, by miles from the resentments and reduced circumstances of the Brexit-supporting communities who feel economically left behind.

Confronted with these figures and this investment logic, many people, and not just in Scotland, will throw up their hands dismissively. Yes, they will say, a retirement income of £50,000 would be very welcome, but my family and I will never amass a million pounds, not in this lifetime or several. Curiously, most Americans, citizens of the richest national economy on earth, would agree: a nice prospect, but a pipe dream. As such feelings are so raw and so common, I was tempted, some years ago, to test the reality of my understanding of home economics, because I, too, had never dreamed, until quite recently, of pursuing an income-doubling strategy.

So I asked one of the families, spawned in part by the same Colorado diaspora, how they had become millionaires several times over. And they told me. And when this husband-and-wife team, now retired professionals, parents of three children, had finished their exposition, both of them sat back on the fine sofa in their spacious North County (San Diego) *hacienda* (3,000–4,000 square feet), and peered at me in wonder. They then confessed that no one – no relation, no friend, no colleague – had ever before asked them how they had succeeded financially. They were mystified at this fact, and therefore astonished by my question.

## SCHMUCKS VS THE PROTESTANT WORK ETHIC

Politeness and respect for privacy may figure in this reluctance to ask about other people's financial circumstances, but more often than not it seems that the people who might learn something really useful about how to make their way in the world financially fail to ask the central question (Why are the rich rich?) because the question itself never occurs to them. Most people are, in this analysis, in a benighted state of ignorance about financial matters. Only much later did I discover that this species of financially hapless person, so often decent and worthy in every other way, is referred to, out of earshot of the domestic staff, by the very wealthy of the New World as a *schmuck*. The term is supposedly Yiddish for 'fool', but in fact it is a term of endearment (and despair) for people who do not know what kind of economy they are living in (aka 'somewhere people').

Sadly, imprudence is not even half of the problem of anyone who cannot find and exploit a profitable niche within the global economy. Let us consider for a moment the financial situation of the greater part of the population of a modern society at retirement age. I will use American statistics because I have them to hand and also because they are inoffensively not Scottish. I thought this might be more tactful when I learned that some Welsh statistical wit has apparently claimed that there are more billionaires and millionaires in the former Occupied Palestinian Territories than in all of Wales. When did the Protestant work ethic die here? When we all stopped going to chapel?

These American statistics make depressing reading. You may have heard the expression 'one-percenters': that is the one per cent of the American population that is composed of billionaires. There is also a substantial army of hundred-millionaires and the like. The net wealth at retirement age for the next four per cent drops as low as our benchmark: one million pounds (to translate airily from dollars in the age of Brexit-inflicted sterling volatility). This income group is sometimes described in the prodigious language of the New World as 'comfortable'. Note that the bottom layer of these four-percenters boast a net wealth of one million pounds, and therefore live 'comfortably' on something approaching £50,000 of income a year. So far, so nothing shocking.

This more or less soothing picture becomes less so, much less so, when we turn to the rest of the population at retirement age: the 95-percenters. Approximately half of this huge body of individuals and families consists of people who insist that the only way they can sustain something approaching their current level of material well-being is to go on working into their late sixties, seventies and beyond. Then even these organized and motivated people will reach some fateful point when they can longer work, and they will slip into the ranks of the other half of these 95-percenters, those who have resigned themselves to an old age of poverty and a falling standard of living from age sixty-five, if not before. To be old is bad enough, but to be old and poor is not something to look forward to after an adult lifetime of labour in the demanding UK economy.

Now let us put these statistics in perspective. Since at least the 1970s, it has become commonplace among the financial advice industry to divide the population not by the value of one's income but by the sources of one's income. This breaks us down into

(1) employees, (2) the self-employed, (3) owners of businesses with employees and (4) the idle rich/independently wealthy who live off their investment income. Some personal financial advisers, including Richard Kiyosawa, controversial financial guru, author of *Rich Dad, Poor Dad* and friend of Donald Trump, have popularized the notion that these four categories are not pigeon holes, bird cages or closed boxes but four linked stages in the financial life-cycle of an individual or family or economic class, such as creatives.

Equip your mind with these organizing principles, this quadrant of categories, and where does it take you? To the sphere of dynamic action in a creative workplace is one answer. This highlights the importance of the 'senior start-up' as discussed in magazines such as *Monocle*. This research calls into the question the stereotypical assumption that most successful entrepreneurs are pushy young people when in fact a typical boss of a new startup is more likely to over 40. The further interesting question is how many of these over 40s are actually over 60. This would be consistent with the thumbnail sketch drawn here of the 'unretired retired' senior citizen of a Remainer as a positive, educated, experienced and ambitious creator of 'the senior start-up'. Significantly, old heads are indeed wiser: senior startups are less likely to fail.

So, according to 'Quadrant Theory' recast in the language of British capitalism, you may start your working life as an employee, and then become a sole trader (recall the army of white van men and women of Cardiff Bay). Then you transform your business into a limited company (preferably with employees to do the frontline work), and finally sell the company as a successful business, thereby generating all or part of that million pounds (or more) in capital mentioned above. *Voila!*

In short, quadrant evolution is a life-cycle. Much of the criticism of gentrification becomes much less persuasive when entrepreneurship is viewed as a life-long quest for creative satisfaction and financial security, so the person who begins this quest as a young but broke creative ends up as a comfortable *rentier*. On this subject there is too much 'black vs white' polemic and too little respect for the huge spectrum of greys. As a result, the social statistician is too often providing perfectly calculated answers to the wrong questions. What tends to be missing in such research and journalism – and not only in Scotland – is the neglected input of what social science calls 'the participant observer': the person who knows what is happening on the ground from direct experience.

## From four per cent to ten per cent

The trick that Scotland and the other Remain nations need to perform is that of transforming the 'comfortable' four per cent into the 'comfortable' ten per cent. In any such income-doubling campaign, it is crucial to recall that of our four income categories, only the employed can lose their jobs because of somebody else's arbitrary decision; the self-employed, the business owner and the independently wealthy are in this regard less vulnerable. These are the five per cent for whom the approach of old age holds few financial terrors. In a greying society, such as Scotland, this distinction may matter, in terms of domestic economy, more than any other, because sooner or later the 95 per cent may need assistance, on a serious scale, from social services, and therefore the Scottish taxpayer.

Several testable rules of thumb follow. First, in principle, one should never work for somebody else (here be not dragons but robots!). Every year you work for somebody else is a year lost when you could be working for yourself and earning more money (the relevant economic concept in play here is 'opportunity costs'). Like success, necessity cannot be argued with; but if you rent from or work for someone else, do it for as short a time as possible. Or, more strategically, use your employment as a springboard for financial success. To consider only one workaday example, it occurs to me in my line of business that every bank lending officer, with that skill set and that customer base, should make it to a million rather easily once he or she quits the bank. So before your high street branch (an MBA course that pays you a salary) closes, prepare for your personal entrepreneurial 'start-up' day.

Second, turn the fact that everyone eventually retires to your advantage. Not as a sad milestone burdened by a lifetime of guilt-driven scrimping and saving to build a modest retirement fund in a bank account but rather as a moment to celebrate the holy grail: a pot of gold that can be earned well before retirement should health, family need, workplace tedium or the robots intrude before you reach sixty-five or seventy. Scour opportunities for self-improvement that reflect a dynamic balance between what you do well and what you can do profitably. Prepare a strategy that takes you as soon as possible from employee to entrepreneur (becoming a sole trader may be a good start). Settle on the *one* thing of a strategy that delivers more life-chances and the highest creative satisfaction, and stick to it until you end up as near as possible to the goal of a decent retirement sustained by investments and a lifestyle business as early in your life as circumstances and ambition allow.

Third, there is another consideration that seems hardly ever to figure in the American discourse on the four quadrants: the implications of all this for those who make and implement public policy or those who are charged with raising the taxes to pay for these policies. For an official or politician tasked with the difficult business of managing Northern Ireland, Scotland or Wales, the Weberian ideal type set out here offers a lifeline in our era of dismal austerity imposed by over-borrowed public finances.

Like Galileo's planets, we must all learn to move if we are to find creative fulfilment, material security and sheltered familial joy. By contrast, the sedentary life is a kind of death, and spiritually always has been. Granted, the path I have proposed here is just one possibility. Better ones will be found, but there must be a new path. The old 'ball-and chain' logic of being stuck somewhere must be abandoned, geographically and mentally. Surely this is the message that counts for those desperately sad communities that voted for Brexit out of despair. Life is a journey. Jesus in the Gospel of John speaks to our condition with scriptural force when he declares: 'Arise! Pick up thy bed and walk.' And, he might have said, then learn to run.

## PART V – THE BREXITEER AS A PERSON: THE ENGLISH NATIONALIST AND SCOTTISH UNIONISM

*Why should the Celtic races, which began with poetry, not finish with criticism?*

— ERNEST RENAN (1896)

### FROM MONEY TO MANNERS

Having got up a great number of Scottish noses in my argument for economic self-improvement and communal salvation, I will now turn from economics to psychology, from money to manners. Again our theme is the relationship of Scottish unionism with English nationalism. It is with the assessment of the Little English national character that the Celtic spirit moves, in Renan's immortal insight, from poetry to criticism. Therefore, I will now attempt something rather unpleasant: an assessment of what I find distasteful and incomprehensible about the national values and philosophic outlook of Little England. I take no pleasure in wielding one of Captain Ahab's barbed harpoons in this way, so the intention is not to malign (what would be the point of that?) but to pursue something more Welsh: our gentle weakness but also our tireless passion for truths near to the bone, in this case a Scottish bone or two. The true target of this exercise has to be Scotland because Little England is impervious to such truths by metaphysical design.

If a Martian anthropologist made a study of the tribes of Brexit Britain, she would very likely conclude that, despite the formidable energies and ambitions exhibited by the Leave nations, Little English men and women appear to lack something: they don't know how to behave. This apparent inability to empathize with other people, to make their concerns my concerns (as I am attempting here with the Scots), to moderate the impulse to speak one's mind on every occasion, this determination always to cause gratuitous offence, and, finally, this endless supping from the barrel of bilious contempt for other cultures, languages and peoples, is quite frankly a bore. What is the Little English problem with being loyal, decent and kind? How mature does a culture have to be before it awakens to the value of these virtues? Is it possible that the Little Englishman is too mean (in both senses), because too green (immature), to share a country with?

Where do Scottish unionists derive the strength and the patience to put up with their fellow unionists among the English Tories who feel compelled to act out in this manner? I personally find it difficult to believe that so many English people suffer from so deeply rooted an inferiority complex and such social awkwardness that this defect of character must be masked by rudeness. So how is one to explain to oneself or others why the first thing an English Wagnerian from Monmouth does when taking his or her seat in the Wales Millennium Centre in Cardiff is to complain loudly, in a cut-glass educated voice, within earshot of a thousand Welsh patriots, that our opera house should not bother with Welsh surtitles? Who do these people think they are?

Whoever they think they are, this gift for rude posturing has political implications. The most subversive foe of the liberties, the communal solidarity, the prosperity, the identity and the material interests of the Scottish unionist who may or may not have voted for Brexit is not the Scottish National Party; it is the revanchist army of Little England. Margaret Thatcher's poll tax experiment so wilfully inflicted on the Scots in 1999 was not an isolated incident. It was a warning shot that the union of England and Scotland was beginning to unravel with the decay of one-nation Toryism.

From the moment the Thatcher government took that clumsy and errant decision up to the sorry hour of David Cameron's successful but half-hearted effort to keep Scotland in the union during the independence referendum, the die was cast. On 23 June 2016, the die stopped rolling, and came up snake eyes for the United Kingdom. The Brexiteer's rejection of the modern world, the implications of which will be examined in the next chapter, makes it obvious why Leave and Remain are not better together. Indeed, we will only be better and stronger when we are apart. The challenge for Scotland is, therefore, to become independent while affirming a unionist link with the only part of England (and the rest of Remain Britain and Ireland) worth having.

WHAT ARE WE TO THEM?

The threat of xenophobic anti-European English nationalism highlights the barbed wisdom of the Machiavellian warning to keep your enemies close and your friends closer. The point of such mortal intimacy in the present context is to ensure that we cultivate an unclouded understanding of the true intentions of our Little English friends who, when push comes to shove, don't give an expedient damn about their friends – or us. If they cared for the survival of the United Kingdom, they would have never inflicted Brexit on us. Hence the paradoxical nightmare that inevitably weighs on the enlightened proponent of unionism – think

of the moderate liberal leadership of Scottish Toryism or the likes
of Nick Clegg's Liberal Democrats: the almost inexplicable habit
of the Brexiteer of closing his eyes to reality as soon as he thinks
his interests are threatened – even when they are not threatened.
This outlook – or lack of outlook, indeed – makes effective government almost impossibly difficult, as demonstrated by so much
that has unfolded since that bitter June day in 2016.

So what are we to them? Where in the Little English mind
is there a sheltered corner to locate a bare minimum of patriotic concern about the well-being of the Celts? Angry and frustrated by a world that will not yield to their rooted conviction
of effortless superiority over Europeans and the rest, the Little
English Brexiteer appears prepared to sacrifice Celtic interests
and requirements at the drop of the proverbial bowler hat. How
else is one to explain the casual callousness of Brexiteer proposals
to sacrifice Welsh and Northern Irish manufacturing and agri-
culture in pursuit of the dream of 'Singapore on the Thames', or
to risk reigniting the Troubles in Northern Ireland to escape the
imaginary tyranny of the European Court of Justice? The potential gain for Brexit England of these fanciful policies in no way
balances out the damage they would inflict on the Celtic nations,
but I fear that too many Englishmen and women do not care.
Perhaps the time has arrived to stop asking them to care.

So, I repeat, what are we to them? The Brexiteer insists on
taking back control of British fishing waters with little interest in
and knowledge of the complex realities of the fishing industry.
Take Shetland, for example, where, as I understand it, more fish
(the devil in the detail rests in the kinds of fish) are harvested and
processed, mainly by workers from the EU, than in the rest of the
UK combined, and mainly for export to the EU. We can catch the
stuff, but we don't eat anything like enough of it. Is there a pattern
here? If the Brexiteer often appears to be indifferent to his own
interests and requirements, indeed often blind to the claims of

reason and good sense, what mortal damage might he inflict on Northern Ireland, Scotland and Wales in a moment of ignorant chauvinist pique? So know your friend; he may be a foul-weather enemy.

## TRAPPED

Much of this problem turns on the question of national character. In search of answers, the Scottish unionist may need to take more car trips with Little English men and women. Beyond the contrivances of public policy and the murky excitement of divisive statistics, Brexit has unleashed something raw and sickening: aroused feelings of *amour propre* and contempt that feed on fierce visions and endless mental churning. Such self-obsession in the Brexiteer yields insights for us. Even before a Little English man or woman begins to hector or belittle, you can recognize one of them by their physical gestures. They invite you into their space, say a living room or a car, and then they proceed to play a kind of parlour game of pushy, tactless one-upmanship.

The warning sign, like the incipit rattle of a desert snake, is the relaxed slither of an arm across the back of a sofa. More menacing still, there is that smug aggressive face that appears above the arm as its passes, in a confident caress, over the back of the front seat of a car as the Little English woman assesses her prey, effectively trapped behind her. I first encountered the Little English slither on a trip back from a conference in Yorkshire in the early 1980s. The English couple, both academics, offered to drive me back to Oxford (thus saving me the rail journey via London).

In my colonial innocence, I thought this was a kindness. But then, while he was driving, she turned back and gazed at me as her long arm travelled across the top of the front seat. With this gesture, as intended, she captured my full attention as I picked up the new, ever so slightly nasty, mood. Then she pounced. 'Tell me,

David, how is it possible the United States has gone from frontier society to decadence so quickly?' I had just met the woman and was stunned by this crass insult. While I pondered whether to give her a verbal slap or just salute her clever-cleverness, it did occur to me that in the reduced hovel of a shack in the poorest county of Mississippi this sort of conduct would be regarded as gross and therefore unthinkable impoliteness. I think the expression is 'not quite civilized'.

It might be comfortingly assumed that the Scots and the Welsh are not quite colonials in the same sense and therefore are normally spared such Little English shallowness. Ambushed too often over the years to entertain this hopeful notion, I found my patience with this snotty superciliousness conclusively exhausted during another car journey, this time from Cardiff to Heathrow. Our 'Home Counties' driver, who had apparently never been to Wales, seemed amicable enough. But he, too, just bided his time until a traffic delay on the M4 gave him his moment to humble the guests from Cardiff Bay sitting in his car. Once the traffic slowed to a halt, his left arm moved across the top of the front seat, and he assumed the expression of an affronted thug: 'Now tell me why the English taxpayer has to pay £30 billion to Wales every year?'

We let this poisonous question hang in the air. The query violated a fundamental British taboo because there is no answer. It was as offensive as talking about a 'frontier' between Wales and England. At that moment, my confidence in the essential unity of the United Kingdom did not die, but the first blow was struck. It prepared me for Brexit. When we arrived at the airport, I offered him an extra £20, which he greeted with a gruff 'What's this for?' I answered: 'It's a Welsh instalment on your tax rebate.'

Any time that suits him, the Little Englishman appears prepared psychologically to pull the plug on the bath (no longer full of coal) of our subsidized financial dependence on London, and this prospect, this simmering danger, reduces Scotland, Wales and

Northern Ireland to the status of hostage states. Today, in our new age of angry direct democracy, the nations of the Celtic Fringe must face up to the implicit demand of the English Brexiteer that they either shut up and do as they as are told (the effective stance of the May government) or be cut off at the knees financially.

This menace is unacceptable. Would any Little Englishman put with up this hostage status for a moment? And, no, I do not believe that there is a convincing Scottish unionist answer to that question. This returns us, by the logic of *force majeure*, to the necessity for partition. And indeed there is no more powerful argument, as we shall see in the next chapter, for partition than England-for-the-English-style ethnic cleansing. Here, in a final word on Scotland and its future, we might observe with truth and feeling that Little England and its Scottish unionist allies find themselves today several planetary systems removed from the dynamic prosperity and good-fellowship of those provinces of our civilized planet governed by the creative classes where healthy technology, inexhaustible talent and inclusive toleration reign over all – and unite us.

WITHERING BEFORE OUR EYES

At one of the more dispiriting moments for Brexiteer resistance to a new referendum, the BBC interviewed an ageing veteran of the campaign to persuade the UK to leave the EU. It was the week when, in the words of Boris Johnson, the dream of quitting the EU seemed to die. This Brexit battle-axe of a political stalwart may have been one of the six 'bastards' who so plagued Prime Minister John Major over the Maastricht Treaty. Whoever he was, I am sure he was a veteran of many car journeys.

Asked for his assessment of the souring state of the British domestic mood, this Brexiteer looked at the interviewer with the worn expression of a weary animal, and muttered: 'I just want to leave.' When I considered the man and his decades-old crusade for national sovereignty and the rest, I longed to help him to a metaphorical door, anywhere in fact where his dream, however unreal, might seem for him somehow real, and therefore his disappointment less of a trial.

And here again we find a delicate mythical insight unfolding. So strange it seems, that after all the centuries, the Celtic soldier of a Scot, now marching fresh out from the mists of antiquity into freedom – the banner of St Andrew in one hand and 'Europa', the blue and gold flag of the EU, in the other – vigorous and bare-chested, seems to have retained his youth, while the Brexiteer, the heir of our erstwhile conquerors, racked with frustration and resentment, appears to age and wither before our eyes as we watch.

# CHAPTER 7

# Fifty shades of ethnic cleansing: Brexit and the defence of Little England

*We are the grandchildren and great-grandchildren of the thousands who came from Ireland to work in our shipyards and our factories. We are the 80,000 Polish people, the 8,000 Lithuanians, the 7,000 each from France, Spain, Germany, Italy and Latvia, and are among the many from countries beyond our shores that we are so privileged to have living here amongst us. We are the more than half a million people born in England, Wales and Northern Ireland, who have chosen to live in Scotland.[5]*

— FROM A SPEECH by Nicolas Sturgeon, in the presence of Her Majesty the Queen, at the opening of the Scottish Parliament, 2014.

*The Los Angeles Police Department have warned the public concerning a threat by Islamic terrorists to kill every US citizen in the city. The authorities fear the death toll may reach as high as nine.*

— A RECENT LOS ANGELINO JOKE

---

[5] Quoted in *Nicola Sturgeon: A Political Life* (2015) by David Torrance.

## OVERTURE - *L'ESPRIT HUMAIN*/THE HUMAN SPIRIT

HIS HAND HOVERED ABOVE ME. His wrist was encased in ecclesiastical lace, which shone in brilliant white as he brought the Host closer. Normally, one waited, kneeling, at the communion rail to be distracted when the priest arrived, either by the holy wafer itself or the glistening polished metal of the communion paten, designed less to catch the Body of Christ should the priest drop it than to remind the communicant of the embodiment of the divine about to be placed on his tongue. But this time something else distracted, for when the priestly voice intoned 'Corpus Christi', the hand that brought the Host to me was black.

It was the same black hand that had, just minutes before, elevated the consecrated Host with the sacred words of Jesus at the Last Supper, in Latin: *Hoc est corpus meum* ('This is my body'). Earlier still, this Jesuit from Uganda had delivered his thoughtful and educating sermon to a packed (and I mean packed) parish church full of repentant Los Angelinos at Lenten tide in an unprepossessing suburban community composed mainly but not exclusively of the diaspora of Europe, Asia and Latin America, thousands of miles from Africa. Such is the universal reach of the Universal Church – and its ability to bind human beings together easily matches that of any empire.

From that transcendent moment, it became impossible for me to conceive of anything of consequence that might separate me, as a human being, from this black priest, a person deserving, certainly in my mind, of undiluted respect and reverence. This inspired encounter, at a crowded twelve o'clock Mass, had been racially prepared for. Not many years earlier, I had been the fussiest of fussy eaters: no sign then of the uncompromising foodie, the victim of *haute cuisine*, into which I metamorphosed much later. My childish refusal to eat drove my parents to despair and finally to our family doctor, a Japanese-American.

This itself was an intercultural miracle because I was born only three years after my father, a landing-craft pilot, had returned from the fierce carnage of the battles of Iwo Jima and Okinawa. The doctor's community, the entire Japanese-American population of Los Angeles, had been forcibly removed, in the winter of 1941–2, from their homes and livelihoods to concentration camps in the far California desert and beyond under the bogus rubric of 'enemy aliens'. A returnee of that now dispersed community of rebuilt lives, this kindly man listened to my mother's anxious concerns, and then held out his hand in gentle restraint. Thence he rose, and took me alone into his inner office, and shut the door. There he addressed me, man to five-year-old man, with medical severity. He told me that unless I learned to eat properly I would die. I listened.

Through such existential encounters, the priest and the doctor became of one substance with me. This chapter on the Brexiteer's call for the democratically authorized ethnic cleansing of the United Kingdom is therefore addressed in a kindly but insistent spirit to those of my fellow countrymen and women who have never experienced the kind of racial epiphanies just described. I am writing for those who, unlike Nicola Sturgeon, would inwardly contest the very notion of a shared *esprit humain*, whose lives have never been sacramentally transformed by moments when one begins to regard people of other lands, creeds and colours not merely as 'DPs' (different people) but as beings as genuinely human as ourselves. With these people we share not just a biological species but also a spiritual condition. This is our common humanity, the living substance of the thing: *Hoc est corpus meum.*

## Part I – The spectre of ethnic cleansing
### Now send them home!
The day after the victory for Brexit in the 2016 referendum, T-shirts appeared suddenly on the streets of Leave Britain declaring: 'We

won the vote; now send them home!' Even in Cardiff, riot-proof police vehicles would soon be seen on the streets with 'Migrant Control' emblazoned over the windscreens. This fierce sentiment and the dark official response conjured up a vision of pandemonium in the mind of anyone who knows anything about world history and modern transport logistics (recall the millions caught on the wrong sides of the border when Greater India was ripped asunder in 1947).

The battle cry 'Now send them home!' tapped into a larger fallacy: the assumption of many, perhaps most, citizens of the United Kingdom, both Leaver and Remainer, elite and non-elite alike, that our departure from the European Union involved something as simple as turning off a light. With a single action, Europe would be gone and we would all be instantly free. The Remainer was trapped by the light-switch metaphor when he or she assumed that the brutal economic consequences of Brexit would begin the day after the referendum vote because we would be leaving the EU on that day. Project Fear was correct about the dangers; it was only wrong about the timing. Note that the global currency traders did respond the day after the referendum and severely punished sterling.

More unnerving is the way so many Leavers cling to the light-switch metaphor: social media is still rife with demands that the UK leave now, today: it will all be not a minute too soon. This entirely unrealistic belief drives many Brexiteers into a barely contained fury. Why have we not thrown that light switch already? Which traitorous cabal in Whitehall and Downing Street is preventing the mass removal of detestable foreigners from our midst for which the electorate of this country voted?

All this passion ignores the fundamental complexities and organic depth of the United Kingdom's place within the European Union, and the many unforgiving implications for British business of any attempt to tear it out. And, to be fair, the ignorance of the angry man in the streets of Leave Britain about the realities of the

European cornerstone of British foreign policy appears to have been shared by almost everyone else – including politicians and news commentators (one suspects that some civil servants knew better, and I am confident that even more scholars understood our true position within the EU). The point is that what we appreciate now about the nature of our complex and binding ties to the European Union reduces the hateful cry 'Now send them home!' to nonsense. The slogan may still be boldly asserted on hundreds of muscle-tight T-shirts, but it is now little more than a national embarrassment, no matter how loudly it is shouted. So why was it nonsense then and why does it remain nonsense now?

The answer can be brought to light by examining a little more carefully what the would-be light-switch thrower really meant with the demand 'Now send them home!'. Were policemen going to start calling on the houses and apartments of Britain's more than three million residents from the rest of the European Union (recall the numbers in Sturgeon's list just for Scotland), with trucks to take thousands of Poles, Lithuanians, Irish, French, Italians and the rest to relocation camps whence they would be moved on to Heathrow, Gatwick and the Channel ports to be put on planes and ferries for expulsion?

The resulting logistical mountain to be climbed defies easy imagining. Were a million and a half British citizens resident in the other member states of the EU suddenly to be sent back to the UK? A simple exercise in addition suggested that perhaps four and half million people would have to be forced into motion 'now'. As a nation, were we going to rip apart thousands upon thousands of families, businesses and homes because a plurality of cranks in Lincolnshire voted for Brexit out of irritation with hearing Albanian spoken on the streets of their community? Against 'Project Fear', might we set 'Project Hate'?

Let us refine this portrait of horror and chaos, of this Dunkirk in reverse, just a bit. The battle cry of 'England for the English' gives us a chillingly precise definition of the 'them' to be sent home. Logically, it means *all* foreigners must leave England. Revealingly, one of the first foreigners to be verbally assaulted in the immediate wake of the referendum result may have been an American on a bus in Newcastle. So, all are to be sent home: all EU nationals and all foreigners from outside the EU (Japanese, Chinese, Americans, Arabs, Russians and Commonwealth passport-holders alike). That is what 'all' means. Our thought experiment in the implications of the impulse to cleanse ethnically becomes still more revealing when we stop resisting the temptation to gloss over the key lacunae in this nightmare vision of pure Englishness: the Scots, the Irish and the Welsh are not English. Or, painfully to sharpen the point, in Wales, Scotland and Northern Ireland the English are Johnny Foreigner.

Imagine, therefore, the response in the Celtic Fringe to the very suggestion, a modest proposal worthy of Jonathan Swift, that several hundred thousand residents here from the Irish Republic might be expelled, be it in a year's time or a fortnight's in a natural extension of the official Home Office policy of enforcing a 'hostile environment' for migration. The idea that Dublin might be tempted to respond in kind and send home its English resident population has never registered on the Brexit mind. The Celts simply do not figure in the Brexiteer's calculations of the English national interest.

We *would* begin to figure if national passions were unleashed in an act of Brexit-inspired madness, and the English ended up being forced to pack their bags in the Republic as well as in Northern Ireland, Scotland and Wales. Illuminated by this fantasy of stark imagining, we may now begin to appreciate, to drill down, in the contemporary idiom, to the true motives behind the demand that we 'take back control'. The point of my exercise in political fantasy is simplicity itself: on the subject of immigration, we need to imagine going over the edge so we can decide *not* to go over the edge. So this chapter has been written to help Leave England make up its mind, once and for all, about what it wants to do with its resident alien population, today and tomorrow. In the meantime, we pray that the violent Brexiteer restrains his hand and assaults no more Spanish tourists with cricket bats or the like, and that Polish residents remain safe from the alt-right Brexit supporters who long to kill them merely for standing in an English street speaking Polish.

FUZZY LOGIC: FIFTY SHADES OF ETHNIC CLEANSING

The term 'ethnic cleansing' sets the pulse racing. It conjures up images of savage human misconduct on a national or communal scale, from the genocide of the Third Reich to the localized slaughter of Srebrenica, with the mass butchery of Rwanda located somewhere in between. But these examples must not encourage us to confuse means with ends. Genocide is a form of ethnic cleansing, but there are other forms. So we must be clear about our methods and our goals in this nasty business of getting rid of foreigners and other communities judged to be intolerable. Whatever the method, the impulse to ethnically cleanse a society is born from the same matrix: the instinctual loathing of foreigners or minorities, either out of fear or out of the urge to subdue them.

This definition is an attempt to address one of the fundamental quandaries of international law: are such exercises in state-sanctioned ethnic cleansing ever legal? The post-Holocaust doctrine of international norms says 'no'. Certainly this was the lesson of the Nuremberg trials. So, one might ask, is the May government's enforcement of a 'hostile environment' against migrants constitutional? Do British courts offer us a shield against such excesses? Without the backbone of European human rights legislation, will this shield become less effective? Hence my resort below to the phrase 'democratically mandated'. Because of the slippery nature of Little English rhetoric, always claiming to be top dog but never owning up to being culpable for anything, I felt it was important to raise the moral temperature somewhat by mobilizing the expression 'ethnic cleansing', and to stretch the concept a bit to cover the demand that a democratic government expel more than three million Europeans who are here legally.

The legal problem – the pursuit of verbal precision and the resort to precedent – is however secondary to a far more fundamental question: What form of 'taking back control' of our borders will satisfy the Brexiteer and persuade him to stop accusing the Remain nations of a 'stab in the back' over immigration? That is not a question of legal philosophy but a matter of national and ethnic self-understanding deformed by contempt and hate. So my definitional experiment is not designed to appease the student of international law but rather to challenge the two old boys on the platform of a Birmingham railway station who, during the World Cup in Moscow, were heard arguing the toss over whether the fortunes of the English national team would have been improved 'without the nig-nogs'.

So will my policy programme outlined here meet the demands of the vast majority of Brexiteers in those areas of England that voted most heavily for Brexit and even now exhibit no fear that a 'no-deal' Brexit might hit their part of Leave Britain very hard? Let us begin with a definition, and then outline an implementation programme for taking back control in the pursuit of the defence of Little England.

> *Democratically mandated ethnic cleansing*: the making of an entire nation ethnically homogeneous, for example, preserving England for the English by legal means.

Consistent with the nationally perceived meaning of Brexit among those who voted for it, democratically mandated ethnic cleansing would be implemented in three stages. First, the current government policy known as the 'hostile environment' would continue until such time as the Kingdom of England becomes officially independent. Consistent with this policy, a climate of fear and uncertainty would be tolerated, indeed fostered and fanned, to encourage non-English EU citizens to leave England voluntarily and not return. To this end, an atmosphere of hostility would be further encouraged among all officials at all levels of government and administration who deal with foreigners (passport control, the police and social services, and all levels of education, including universities). Passport rules and the like would be strictly enforced to generate conspicuous examples of arrest, jail sentences and deportation. Public demonstrations of anti-foreign feeling would enhance this climate of fear, as would random acts of violence (murder, beatings and verbal abuse). Until the establishment of the KE as a state on its own, no existing work contracts with non-English citizens would be renewed, to create more jobs for English people. At the same time, official preparations would begin at all levels of state-provided social services to receive the English citizens who may be expelled from other EU countries in response to this hostile environment or who may feel newly unwelcome, or just anxious, as residents abroad.

Second, after independence for the KE, it would become illegal for any non-English person (that is, any foreigner, including both non-EU and EU citizens, as well as all citizens of the UKF) to reside, to work or to make any form of purchase, including the buying or renting of property, in the Kingdom of England. These prohibitions would be enforced by black passporting, as would the denial of all access to social services (including public housing), state education and the NHS.

Third, from the date of the birth of the Kingdom of England (or as soon as practical thereafter), the borders of the country would be closed to all foreigners indefinitely. The only exceptions would be foreigners in transit or those caught up in dire emergencies (automobile accidents, sudden severe illness and the like). Furthermore, after independence a universal consensus would be achieved, from the neighbourhood up, on whether the word 'English' might officially and universally be used, at all levels of society, to apply to residents of the KE who are not white or who are of mixed race. We need a settled judgement, agreed by all as a nation, on this subject.

Are you clearer now about what you want and why? On this subject, I propose to entertain no Little English fuzziness ('I want what I want but there must be no adverse consequences for me') or sentimentality ('I want them to go but I like my French neighbours') or opportunism ('I only want to get rid of the Albanian riff-raff'). No, here I will offer only strict, consistent and unclouded clarity. These are pitiless things you are insisting our benighted country do, so we must be clear: a lot clearer and more honest than many of you have been so far.

We may need to learn, therefore, to tread more carefully around or stamp more firmly on the Little English hypocrisy at work in the minds of those two old boys in Birmingham, because – it being Birmingham – one old boy might stoically concede that one of his granddaughters is married to a mixed-race boy ('Lovely lad, really'), while insisting on his right as an Englishman to speak his mind with his mates down at the pub about 'Pakis', as one does in Birmingham.

More to the piercing point, it may be well past time for candour about the true heart of darkness in all of this: the suspicion that the person who finally needs to be listened to very carefully so as to be perfectly understood, and then convincingly appeased, is Tommy Robinson, leader of the English Defence League. Such appeasement may be essential if partition is to work and the Kingdom of England is to cohere across all fifty shades of the ethnic cleansing that provides it (them, you) with its true *raison d'être*. Unsparing clarity: isn't Welsh realism fun?

## PART II – HITLER'S JIBE: 'A STAB IN THE BACK'

In the Little English mind, anti-European xenophobia is never that far removed from the English problem with race, as well as the widespread assumption that the English are superior to all other peoples, and that this superiority must be ritually manifested at all levels of English life so that all non-English people here know their place. In all these considerations, there is one destination – legally, morally, practically – to which we must not allow the Leave voter to take us. Nor must we allow them, worse still, to blame us with Hitler's jibe ('stab in the back') should the red-white-and-blue bulldog of English patriotism feel fatally betrayed because his hopelessly inflated expectations for Brexit are finally frustrated.

A raking light is cast on this dark place (think of Joseph Conrad) in the secret tapes recorded by Detective Mark Fuhrman, a policeman with neo-Nazi interests and sympathies (Did he really have a taste for Richard Wagner?) who was a key figure in the trial of the famous US footballer O. J. Simpson. Those interested in this extraordinary legal battle might want to watch Netflix's film *American Crime Story: The People versus O. J. Simpson.* Here, however, all we need to know is what this Los Angeles policeman's true feelings were about how to exploit (and abuse) the authority of the police to serve the cause of communal ethnic cleansing.

In a set of interviews later submitted as evidence in court, Fuhrman describes how to eliminate 'Niggers' (his word) from 'White' communities. This example of ruthless frankness offers a limit case, a polar extremity, against which to set and measure the varied range of anti-racial feelings – hence the phrase 'fifty shades' – that prevail in Brexit Land (and beyond). In short, Brexiteers must be forced to choose between living in a state with a liberal government where pernicious, illiberal attitudes and practices are combated at almost every turn, and a state of their own free of potential victims of such racial and ethnic abuse. In short, the hope is that a partition of the UK into Leave and Remain nations will make the Brexiteer ethnic cleanser less disturbed by foreigners on the streets of the Kingdom of England because there will not be any. Would Tommy Robinson be content with this state of affairs? We need to ask him, and I mean that seriously.

The goal is to ensure that every KE racist is as content as possible with the new ethnically cleansed state of affairs: every single one. So suddenly we have arrived at a pure vision of Little England. This vision provides one of the most important rationales for Brexiteers to have a home of their own, a place where they are so comfortable in their skins that the temptations to embrace the views of a Mark Fuhrman will be reduced as closely as possible to nought. And, in exchange, the Remainers must have a home where the Brexiteer will not make us uncomfortable because he and his kind will be safely located elsewhere. So no more talk of a stab in the back; fair enough?


How the EDL trumps the fifty shades

A little more pressure now needs to be applied to the idea of 'fifty shades' of democratically mandated ethnic cleansing. Despite this variety of kinds and degrees of racism and xenophobic feelings, certain things may be asserted with confidence about life as it is lived in the UK today. For example, I am sure that no elite spokesman or woman for the Brexit cause with a seat in Parliament would personally kill a West Indian Briton, an American or a Pole (or, for that matter, a pro-Remain MP) found innocently walking the streets of his or her constituency, or hire someone to do so.

I am equally confident that no senior Brexit politician, particularly in the Tory Party, would applaud someone who committed an act of violence against a black Briton, American or Pole in his or her constituency. One would probably have to concede, in the name of realism, that the stereotypical Little Englishman might still resort to ritual verbal humiliation of non-English people in order to remind those non-English people who is in charge here in Britain. But what the politician, however influential or highly regarded, cannot do is to guarantee that every member of his constituency, without exception, will refrain from the aggressive abuse of his fist, his baseball bat or her voice against foreigners and ethnic minorities.

For this reason, when and if the Leave and Remain nations agree to partition, all the potential victims of this kind of persecution and abuse will be encouraged to abandon Leave Britain for the tolerance and acceptance of the Remain nations. This is of course an anticipatory gesture, because almost certainly all foreigners would be compelled to leave every area of the UK that voted for Brexit. Before the 'Windrush' scandal, I would have assumed that Britons of Asian, African or West Indian descent, to cite the principal categories at issue, would have been legally and realistically secure in Leave areas if they had either been born here or become naturalized citizens of this country. Today, after Windrush, this hopeful picture is less than certain, and therefore here again I would emphasize that, as part of the treaty of partition, the Remain nations would offer sanctuary to all these potential victims, British-born or naturalized, of the 'hostile environment'. You would have a secure home with us.

This elaborate, complex, expensive and disturbing programme of finding new homes for those displaced by partition would serve not one but two purposes. First, it would put all the non-English people no longer welcome in new Kingdom of England out of harm's way. Their safety, dignity and material well-being would thereby be secured. Second, to amplify the point made earlier, Leave England would, in principle, be inhabited only by unmistakably ethnic English people, and so the Brexiteer with his ingrained xenophobic tendency would be that much less likely to succumb to the hard racial logic of the EDL. If the kind of partition I am proposing is achieved and the Kingdom of England is ethnically transformed (for better or worse, depending on your perspective), the EDL might be persuaded to fold its tent and organize a final party to celebrate its victory in its new *Liberal-freie Heimat.*

## WHY ALL ROADS LEAD TO PARTITION

In *Tinker, Tailor, Soldier, Spy,* John Le Carré includes a scene in a bar near Fleet Street. This small slice of London background and social commentary does not advance the deliciously convoluted plot in any way but it does feed the author's other motive for writing fiction: political and social criticism. Certainly Le Carré's *en passant* observation serves our purposes here. This is a moment towards the end of the book, when Smiley arrives to catch Jerry Westerby by surprise (like an investigating police officer). Westerby is an endearing hack of a journalist, and the paper he writes for is governed, in Le Carré's view, by a double editorial principle: 'Short sentences; facile opinions'. Westerby is also an unsuspecting innocent employed by the Circus to gather information on life behind the Iron Curtain. In this bar, where Westerby and Smiley talk about 'Czecho', there is some local colour:

> At the bar a florid man in a black suit was predicting the imminent collapse of the nation. He gave us three months, he said, then curtains.

Moments later, over the hubbub of the bar, the voice of the pessimist again catches Smiley's attention:

> 'Trouble is,' the florid man at the bar was saying, over the top of his drink, 'we won't even know it's happened.'[6]

---

[6] Published in 1974

Sentences short or long, facile or ignorant, announced in beery breath or otherwise, are not the point. Finally, the issue turns on the assumption that an Englishman has the right to hold his views and speak them freely. He cannot be compelled to do otherwise. That is the other point, and indeed the larger and more salient point, of the judge's intervention in the trial of David Irving affirming Holocaust denial when sincere. True, the climate of national opinion affects this right, or tries to. Political correctness and legislation to curb the public expression of inflammatory sentiments against this group or that have narrowed the scope of this right of an Englishman to speak his mind. But one must see that the impact of political correctness as a correction of the national discourse, whether in the press or in the pub or on the web, has provoked a counter-push.

This ingrained defence of an Englishman's right to speak his mind, be he Sir Humphrey or Alf Garnett, is the source of the most important blow delivered to the British state by the Brexit referendum: the elevation of pub talk to a constitutional principle. I am not being glib here. Quite the contrary: direct democracy, referendums and the like, subvert the spirit and the letter of the British constitution because our political tradition has been, certainly from the American vantage point, one long conspiracy to prevent the opinions of ordinary people from directing state policy – until, that is, June 2016.

The intention behind the way indirect or representative democracy functions is in no way malign; quite the contrary, it is essential to the effectiveness of parliamentary government. In effect, a deal has been struck. Elections allow the electorate to 'throw the incompetents out' in the language of the polite vernacular, and this electoral function thereby gives broad direction to state policy. But the division of political labour in an indirect democracy, where we select our Members of Parliament and then leave them to manage the day-to-day affairs of state, encourages a form of intellectual apartheid: the ordinary man in the street (or the pub) may entertain any view of the state of the nation ('He gave us three months') in perfect freedom because there are no direct policy consequences of his speaking his mind. He may know a great deal about politics, but in principle he does not have to know anything. His ideas about things never bang up against reality.

If one then factors in the truth that the English as a nation are served by precious few specifically English political institutions (because the functions of government are subsumed under a British system of rule), one sees that the electorate as an electorate is never disciplined into the burdens and responsibilities of direct self-government. Government, in an indirect democracy, is the job of the elite. This is why the Englishman's right to speak his mind on any subject remained entirely undisturbing until June 2016. Then, the English people had their say, and our elites, in parliament and elsewhere, found their constitutional function subverted. The opinions of the pub-goer ('short sentences; facile opinions') became, as it were, state policy. The result has not been a replay of the Peasants' Revolt of 1381 but something much more momentous: what the Middle Ages might have called our 'Peasant Revolution', something with which the modern British political system is entirely ill-equipped to cope. Does this not offer us a cogent explanation of the political floundering of the May government and parliament since the Brexit vote?

If I am even half right about the elevation of pub talk to a constitutional principle, the British state as it is presently organized must be reconceived or abandoned. This is because the forceful, illiberal and ill-informed pub orator has become the legitimating organ of British government. We cannot live together governed by this salt-of-the-earth intolerance from below. On this subject, Welsh realism urges us to accept the fact that if the Little Englishman is genuine in his racism and xenophobia, we cannot easily influence him to alter his beliefs. And if he will not abandon his testing and testy national outlook, we must allow him to go his own way, and we must go ours.

Perhaps in the end, a Kingdom of England will give the Brexiteer the air to breathe freely, and to air his prejudices with a proud 'hurrah' anytime he chooses. This Kingdom of England would also confront him directly with the political, economic and moral consequences of this right to speak his mind, and all that will follow from it. And there would be social consequences. This whitewashed purity of a part of England strictly reserved only for the English would be free of Celts. Every Welsh-speaking Welsh person, every kilt-wearing Scot, every Mass-going Irishman would be encouraged to remove himself and his family from harm's way in this Brexit England so that the illiberal Brexiteer of an Anglo-Saxon, no matter what shade of ethnic cleanser he was, will feel that he is the absolute master of all he surveys, and therefore be content.

'Control', that key word in the promise of the Brexit campaign slogan, would thereby be reasserted, in every sense that matters. Of course, even in Remain Land, foreigners would be vulnerable to verbal or physical abuse merely because they are foreigners; but the prudent calculation would be that the chances of their being threatened or humiliated at the passport control desk, in the strip-search room, in the police station or in the courts will be much, much less in Remain Britain and Remain Northern Ireland. But finally we must all be where we want to be – even the old boys on that station platform in Birmingham.

OUR ISLAND STORY

Little England, their Little England: what would George Orwell make of it now? My Irish-American mother had a suspiciously grand English acquaintance, a spiritual heir of the Protestant ascendancy over Catholic Ireland, who detested the trappings and forms of the Irish Republic. When we occasionally met her, this acquaintance conspicuously refused even to attempt to pronounce the proper Gaelic title of the Irish prime minister. So instead of 'the Taoiseach', she said 'The Tea Shop', having tightened her face with a slight clever-clever *moue* of Little English contempt.

This attitude is a curt echo of that revelation of the quality of mercy exposed in the nineteenth century when thousands of Irish men, women and children were dying in the blighted potato fields. During that grim hour, the Londonderrys, the fabulously wealthy scions of the ascendancy in Ulster, who apparently were spending the then unimaginably large sum of £150,000 rebuilding their magnificent ancestral estate in County Down, offered thirty morally strained pounds towards famine relief. I hope they *thought* that at least it was something, but I doubt it.

This patronizing executive attitude of our former masters is still active in the politics of Brexit. Take, for example, the frequently made demand that the UK government, acting solely in the interests of Little England, should punish the Irish Republic – Jacob Rees-Mogg, not the worst offender in this regard, has urged the May government to ruin Irish dairy and beef producers by banning imports into Great Britain – until Dublin stops resisting Brexiteer wilfulness over the border between Northern Ireland and the Republic. The English MP for North Somerset fails to mention that such a ban would be equally ruinous for dairy and meat producers in Northern Ireland. I suspect, like the Londonderrys, he may not care. As a Brexiteer, Rees-Mogg wants what he wants, and that is the end of the matter (for him, not us).

So what we are left with is merely the most recent expression of the old high-handed imperiousness that inflicted the long, bloody nightmare of the imperialist, colonialist and settler oppression, from Elizabeth I to Ian Paisley (think back to the violent ethnic cleansing of West Belfast in 1967, when Jack Lynch almost dispatched Dublin's army across the border to protect the North's oppressed Catholic minority), that got us into this mess in the first place. This now *passé* form of supercilious superiority will no longer do, because it encourages the English nationalist to try to evade an inescapable choice: Brexit or the sovereign unity of the United Kingdom?

This bellicose aggressiveness in which the Little Englander takes such pride has once again become an intolerable defect in every sense but one. Hitherto the rest of Britain has put up with this neo-colonialist hubris towards the Celtic Fringe. Now perhaps at this turning point in 'our island story' it may be time to apply some Welsh realism working in tandem with some philosophical thoroughness to expose the true sources of Brexiteer resentment and intolerance, before we consider how these defects of temper might be remedied. The remedy I have in mind is the old-fashioned Christian virtue of kindness. One of the magical effects of this metaphysical probing will be the transformation of the Irish Question into what it really is: the English Question.

THE KINDNESS OF STRANGERS

Near the end of his long, distinguished and prolific life as a novelist and critic, Henry James was asked (this story, almost mythical, comes in more than one version) what lessons he drew from his experience of life. The question was posed in a public forum, and James apparently paused at first to reflect, and then offered what he thought was the wisest lesson a person might glean from human existence, and that was to be kind. The American writer's interlocutor was not quite content with this response, and did not know James well, so he persisted, and asked: 'Was there anything more the Master might recommend?' Now I suspect the man with the question had James's full attention, and the aged author probably focused his gaze on the young man, paused once more for effect, and replied (I paraphrase): 'Yes, there are three things that I commend to you to learn and practise in your life as a person: Be kind, be kind, be kind.'

How does one person teach another to be kind? What does it take for one human being to set aside the deeply schooled feelings of hostility, fear, prejudice and contempt that may surface when he is confronted with a person who speaks a different language, wears a different coloured skin, is sexually attracted to his own gender, or worships a different God or none? Let me apologize for offering two vignettes from my life to make the point vivid. They are both Welsh vignettes, and it is salient to ask why Welsh stories might matter as much as they do (or should) in an Irish context. The answer is in the telling.

When my husband and I became civil partners (we married later on Bora-Bora), in a brief ceremony at Cardiff City Hall, two of our straight neighbours, who had been our witnesses, took us to lunch in a restaurant in the Bay. When this magical meal concluded, something else magical happened. In settling our account, the waitress asked if we were celebrating a special occasion (the bill was that large), and when we told her, she said: 'Just wait, please. Don't leave yet.' She disappeared only to return almost immediately with a chilled bottle of champagne, a gift from the staff and the restaurant. We were overwhelmed by this act of thoughtful solidarity. I was quite weepy.

The contrasting incident occurred on a trip to Zimbabwe. My husband and I were staying, with slight trepidation, at a grand colonial-era hotel near the Victoria Falls. The place was a time capsule from the 1930s. We appeared to be the only gay couple in this large, rambling hotel in a country where to be homosexual is illegal. The staff treated us with gentleness and immaculate courtesy, despite the lingering atmosphere of imperial class-mindedness and Victorian intolerance. The residents of the hotel were another matter. The colonial formality, the liveried servants and the nearly endless array of portraits of crowned heads encouraged the visiting Brits, almost all of a certain age and outlook, to carry themselves with strained superiority and loftiness. It was like turning up to the wrong drinks party in Monmouth.

One evening –the sunsets were beautiful – my husband strolled ahead of me into one of the grand salons, and so I encountered on my own (a punishment for dawdling) the glaring basilisk eye of a rather miserable-looking Englishman, fierce moustache and all, who was not happy to see us. His aged wife did not look thrilled either. This sort of encounter is so rare nowadays, at least where we live, that I just glanced away to avoid any unpleasantness. So as I walked past, his voice, and his message, reached me from behind: 'Filthy queer!' he spat out with a slight lisp. This moment was not magical.

Now tell me, which person – the girl with the champagne bottle or the man with the basilisk eye – voted for Brexit? I will bet you, in perfect confidence, and I am not a betting man, that any reader of this story can tell who voted for what and why without any scope for error. The certainty involved verges on the infallible. So what I want to learn from this poll of the obvious is simple: what are the reasons why I would want to share a country with him rather than with her? Is there any doubt involved in this choice between a discourteous bigot and a female miracle of human sympathy?

When you have answered, we can proceed to the true point of the story: how did this miracle of gentle thoughtfulness come to be? What made her capable of spontaneous acts of what, in a different context, Tennessee Williams called 'the kindness of strangers'? Beginning with Ireland, this cult of human sympathy and tolerance is gradually becoming the ruling philosophy of humanity across the Celtic Fringe and the proud march of great cities that form the backbone of Remain England.

Looking back now to the way in which so many Britons, like our cousins in the Irish Republic, have become kinder and more tolerant, it seems to me that the radiant life and tragic death of Princess Diana may have marked a decisive turning point in the emotional life of our country, and helped to make us what we are now. We do not propose to change. In this way, a climate of kindness, openness and mutual solidarity is taking root, gradually but genuinely, across the whole of Ireland, Scotland, Free Wales and Free England. Nietzsche urged human beings to become what they are, and we Remainers are ready to become what we are. And so, I fear, is Little England. Pity about the difference, but the final truth of the matter is that some places are kinder, more decent and more civilized. So make your choice.

# CHAPTER 8

# A call to arms: Brexit, America's vital centre and the global defence of liberal civilization

*We have it in our power to make the world over again.*
*My world is my country, all mankind are my*
*brethren, and to do good is my religion.*
*I believe in the equality of man; and I believe that*
*religious duties consist in doing justice, loving mercy,*
*and endeavouring to make our fellow creatures happy.*

— THOMAS PAINE (1737–1809), English-born
American patriot and uncompromising
defender of the European Enlightenment

## A MANIFESTO: BREXIT AND AMERICA'S VITAL CENTRE

On 8 November 2016, I found myself in a bar near Mendocino, on California's Pacific coast, watching the election returns. My husband and my friends from Oakland who were dining in the adjoining room could not bear to watch this dismal televised spectacle, so I was condemned to walk to and fro relaying the sour news as one northern industrial state after another fell to Donald Trump, and America elected its first demagogue as president. The only comfort I took that evening while I was absorbing this blow was that I was in one of my favourite places on earth: the northern Californian wine and *haute cuisine* country is an enchantment that extends, in my experience, northwards from Napa and Sonoma, across the Russian River, then up the coast to Little River and Mendocino.

So, thousands of miles from my home in Cardiff Bay I may have been, but I nevertheless felt surrounded by people who shared my political ideals, my cultural outlook and my philosophy of life. However grim the hour, it was good to be among them, knowing that I could have found the same comforting community gathered in mourning that evening in a thousand bars and restaurants not only in America but across Canada, Europe, Australia, New Zealand, and every other vital centre and precious outpost of liberal civilization. To adapt a famous observation from Flaubert, on that evening 'I was not a man, I was a world'.

We are a world, perhaps half a billion strong, and growing. Two of the pillars of this world are liberal America and the Remain nations of the United Kingdom. In 2016, that *annus horribilis*, we chose sides: the vital centre of the United Kingdom and America voted for liberal democracy, free markets and the creative class's 'Four Ts'. This vital centre included liberals and social democrats as well as gays, the young, thinking ethnic and religious minorities, the university-educated, artists and intellectuals, hard-core creatives, civilized urbanites, unrepentant Sixties radicals and, on the western side of the Atlantic, a remarkable innovation: enlightened nationalists. They all voted by decisive margins for Europe and against Trump. Our technological dream has given the world the technical marvels of the twenty-first century; that same technology has given us the boiler rooms of Big Brother and the 'dark web', spreading denial of the Holocaust and other pernicious lies. In this sense, 2016, one of the worst years in the history of liberal civilization since Hitler came to power in 1933, was a profound moment of self-discovery and self-realization. Now we know what is to be done.

Those who had given insufficient thought to the matter previously now seized on the political potential of the creative classes, while the creative classes themselves finally realized that they form the backbone of the vital centre of the West's two largest English-speaking liberal democracies. These are the confident, pay-your-own way taxpayers who are at once eco-friendly, techno-friendly, open-minded and optimistic to a fault. But the newest imperative of the vital centre and the creative classes may prove to be the most unexpected and the most important. And that is this: to keep safe this world in which we so enjoy living, we are going to defend it against the enemies of truth and facts, of knowledge and enlightenment. The new enemies of the Open Society are what Voltaire called the 'obscurantists' (the Darth Vaders of the dark web), along with Marx's 'sacks of potatoes' (the flat-earth provincial and bigoted couch potatoes), the depressed and the resentful, the pirates and the poor, the billionaire robber barons and the opiate-dependent underclass on both sides of the Atlantic.

If Franklin D. Roosevelt (who would not have lost an election against Donald Trump) once called America 'the arsenal of democracy', today liberal America must be our 'fortress of democracy'. In this struggle with the dark web, the hate-mongers and the populist racists, America's vital centre is as indispensable to us on the world stage as Free England is to the United Kingdom Federation. If this America can rally to the cause of liberal civilization, we here in Europe will do the same. We will assume the burden of the greater defence with our brothers and sisters across Europe. Where once there was hesitancy because of this or that tragic memory, we shall persuade them to shed their fears and pick up their shields. Our hour has arrived. It is time for a call to liberal arms.

THE DEFENCE OF LIBERAL CIVILIZATION: THREE QUESTIONS
ON THE WAY TO A PLAN OF ACTION

*Ask not what your country can do for you; ask what you can do
for your country.*
— PRESIDENT JOHN F. KENNEDY (1961 Inaugural Address)

### 1. Is the question of partition the decisive question facing America and the United Kingdom?

After all the controversies, all the accusations and all the unhappiness before, during and after the referendum vote on Brexit and the election of Donald Trump to the US presidency, only partition can conclusively overcome the political deadlock that now grips the United Kingdom and the United States. If partition is rejected, we must have compromise. So what are you and your political faction prepared to sacrifice, what 'red lines' or points of political principle are you prepared to negotiate in order to preserve the unity and the effective government of your country? Because if you are not prepared to countenance any such compromises, the only serious practical option is partition: the creation of two nation-states where there is now only one. If you want a new country that embodies all the principles that matter to you, and only those principles, it can be done. The Wisdom of Solomon can still win the day. Thus, partition would spare us; it would spare us each other. So love your country by compromising or leave it: abandon it for what you truly want so you will be content.

### 2. If Americans no longer have the will and the means to defend democratic Europe from its regional enemies, how can we Europeans protect ourselves?

In 2015, a television series titled *Okkupert* ('Occupied') was broadcast on Norwegian television. Conceived by a creative team led by Karienne Lund, Jo Nesbø and Erik Skjoldbjærg, the story envisions a Russian military occupation of Norway. The plot is set implausibly in motion by the contrived idea of an arm-wrestle between Oslo and the EU over how to protect the environment from oil-drilling pollution in the North Sea, but much the most important twist in the plot involves neither Oslo, nor Moscow, nor Brussels. The twist is this: the United States refuses to protect Norway although that country is a member of NATO. A year after the programme was broadcast across the European Union, Donald Trump as president-elect publicly aired his doubts about America's commitment to defend western Europe from external aggression under Article 5 of the NATO treaty.

Since the inauguration of President Trump, the depth and firmness of American treaty obligations to defend Japan and South Korea, as well as western Europe, have been called into doubt more than once, only to be reaffirmed hours or days or weeks or months later. America's promise to defend us here in Europe is, in a manner all too typical of the Trump administration, being winked and nudged to death. Those Europeans who have desperately searched for a silver lining in this diplomatic debacle think they have found one. This silver lining offers no comfort; just clarity. Mr Trump's now-you-see-it, now-you-don't commitment to NATO reflects his gambler's awareness of how rapidly Washington's pile of chips on the table is diminishing. The weight of America's national debt is that great.

What if it is true that the United States can no longer afford to defend us, today or tomorrow, as generously as it has in the past? Or, what if American voters are no longer bothered by the growing defence challenge that Moscow and Beijing pose to western Europe as well as Japan and South Korea? If the United States cannot or will not defend us, the question who will look after us roars into life. In short, is Mr Trump merely highlighting a problem that will survive him?

With the security of half a billion people living in 28 democracies inside the European Union at stake, what are we to do?

We must have a reliable and enduring solution. One such answer would be for us to signal to Moscow that we are willing to become a Russian satrap or protectorate. This question is not rhetorical, because Mr Putin may be the most gifted and far-sighted geo-political thinker to hold the highest authority since John Paul II assumed the papal throne in 1978. Leadership of this calibre plays for the highest stakes; the Pope who helped to free Poland from communist rule and thus bring down the Soviet Union is not called St John Paul the Great for nothing. So I that recommend that Mr Putin be neither underestimated or carelessly mocked by his liberal critics.

Mindful of all this, I am confident that if the EU can gird its loins, we can transform the door of diplomatic weakness that the Master of the Kremlin is exploiting into a sturdier wall of pan-European protection. In this effort, history is our ally. Given their brutal experiences under Stalin and his heirs, what will the Balts – or, for that matter, the Romanians, Czechs, Slovaks and, by natural extension, the Finns – make of this prospect of Russian hegemonic domination? Then there are the impossible Poles and the pushy Hungarians. Is somebody in Warsaw and Budapest forgetting 1945, 1956, 1958 and the fate of people such as József Cardinal Mindszenty? Indeed, what will all of Europe, from Helsinki and Riga to Malta and Lisbon, feel about the return of Russian subjugation? And yes, complain about Putin's geostrategic brilliance all you like, but we still must have a solution to our exposed defences.

Confronted with Moscow's clarity of purpose and diplomatic resolve, our only proper option comes vividly and persuasively into view: we must create a Fortress Europe, one capable of defending our borders against all comers while allowing us to project our power so that we can act as an irresistible force for good in Africa and the Middle East. It might also be sensible for this new Fortress Europe to assume naval patrol duties to guard trade routes across the North and South Atlantic so that we can properly share part of these regional naval responsibilities with the United States, along with our partners and allies in Africa and Latin America.

In building, financing, leading and manning the walls of our Fortress Europe, the United Kingdom Federation would play its full part. And, freed of the Euro-hate wing of the Leave nations, partition would encourage us to make rather a good fist of it. Our defence muscle would certainly make a difference to Europe's future, and we would certainly be punching well above our weight. We Europeans would indeed be one of the world's select few superheavyweights, and therefore no longer a power or collective of powers to be threatened, exploited or abandoned.

For a policy of detente *vis-à-vis* Moscow to succeed, we would have to be prepared to match or exceed Russia's still impressive nuclear arsenal (this will require careful thought and much discussion) and formidable cyber-warfare capabilities, as well as its large conventional forces. At the same time, the EU would need to engage Russia constructively across a wide spectrum of shared defence interests and peacekeeping responsibilities. The result might be a new Cold War balance of power without the cold (or America), but we can make this work because necessity demands it.

Russia will still be there after Putin. Furthermore, even while he is charge of the Russian Federation I suspect he will be interested in designing and managing a future that is good and secure for his country after he is gone because Russia remains so obviously part of Europe. But then, Russians are Europeans; Peter the Great, Tolstoy, Tchaikovsky, Mandelstam and Solzhenitsyn made them so. Indeed, when the State Hermitage Orchestra, that magnificent collection of soloists, performs Mozart and Prokofiev, surrounded by the genius of Venetian painting in the Hermitage's Italian salon, Europe and Russia are one. Upon the supreme greatness of this shared cultural heritage and moral experience, we can build a common future. And, with the wavering in Washington, we need to.

### 3. 'There are no facts; only interpretations.' Was Nietzsche right?

If democracy is, as Clement Attlee proposed, government by discussion, why are we no longer listening to each other? Under the lash of Brexit and the Trump presidency, public discussion of many of the most momentous issues confronting the UK and the US has disintegrated into a shouting match. In the UK, the public airing of popular opinion on once prestigious programmes such the BBC's *Question Time* has been reduced, since the Brexit referendum, to an Orwellian 'hate rally'. On social media, the British have proceeded down the bitter path of mannerless, unrestrained invective and fact-free argument pioneered in America. In the process, the internet has become an echo chamber of our worst fears and suspicions. So, finally, at this late hour, we must embrace Max Weber's famous political insight into the cautionary restraint contained in objective truths: there are always inconvenient facts for any political position, mine no less than yours. Such facts are true, objective and therefore cannot be wished away because they are inconvenient.

## END GAMES: BREXIT AND GOD'S VIEW OF REALITY

The American debate over the impact of a trade war that sets the United States against China, Japan and South Korea as well as Canada and the EU is in essence an argument over anticipatable consequences: if we impose import duties, others may do the same, with potentially severe repercussions for the exporters involved. By British standards, the American debate, however erratic because Mr Trump is the prime mover, has been relatively rational: consequences are weighed and remedies considered; perhaps then ignored, but at least they are considered.

In contrast, the Brexiteer revels in the idea of the UK falling out of the EU single market. He welcomes it with absolute confidence because of his blind belief that there will be no negative consequences. Reality consists of what the Brexiteer wants, and only what the Brexiteer wants. The Brexiteer appears to believe (the word 'think' is too strong here), for example, that his country is immune to the impact of market forces. The failure of the Brexit advocate to make proper sense of the rules and practices governing global trade under the rules of the World Trade Organization is simply baffling – and dangerous.

This stance, as I noted earlier, is based on the obscure premise that underwrites this rejection of reality. This premise is not just another example of superficial political mindlessness, but rather something metaphysical: the astonishing Little English assumption, grounded in a categorical misunderstanding of Anglo-American philosophy, that reality consists only of what I want (this is not a Welsh idea). Does this disconcerting premise strike anyone as vaguely familiar on the other side of the 'Pond'? It should do, because it was American advocates of Anglo-American philosophy who tactlessly endorsed the key lacuna in Brexit metaphysics: the assumption that objective reality does not exist and therefore reality consists of nothing more or less than my subjective preferences. This is why the Leaver thinks that his or her desires are reality (the rest of us don't get a look in).

In the hands of the delusional Brexiteer or American gun advocate, this metaphysical dogma is the stuff of political disaster. Note further, in a delicious irony, that the anti-intellectualist authoritarians and contemporary heirs of the 'know nothings', who refuse to be to be tamed by any notion of reality beyond the reach of their own preferences, including all bodies of inconvenient fact and anticipatable consequences, would cheerfully shut Oxford or Harvard, to name the two universities most culpable and most vulnerable in this dreadfully dispiriting business. The rational coherence of Churchill's English-speaking democracies now hangs by the thinnest of metaphysical silk threads.

## No subservience: a God's-eye view of economic reality

As both the Brexit vote and the election of Donald Trump were, at many points, delayed electoral reactions to the Great Recession that began in 2008–9, let us examine the predictable but brutal consequences of that episode that we avoided only by the skin of our economic teeth. The true character of this fraught experience may come as news to far too many people who should have known better; but then we were all travelling hopefully. On the day Lehman Brothers collapsed I was on holiday in Italy. When I heard the news in Lucca, I had to go back to my hotel room and lie down. My fears for the financial health of the world over the next weeks and months were that great.

## No more winking at economic reality

What did all this mean in human terms? Thousands of people around the world lost their jobs and almost everyone suffered some form of financial anxiety. The political, economic and social consequences – austerity and the reaction to austerity, mistrust of elites and the free market and an underlying mistrust of globalization in all its forms, particularly immigration and the free movement of people, are frequently traced, consciously or instinctually, to the Great Recession of 2008–9. It has become a clichéd defence of the Brexiteer's desire to leave the EU without a deal to say that the dangers should be compared to the damp squib of the so-called 'Millennium Bug'; but the better analogy (not exact, but better) for the variety of threats posed by an abrupt 'no-deal' UK departure from the single market is another 'Black Friday'in slow motion.

The potential dangers of Britain suddenly falling out of the European Union have been consistently ignored until very recently. The economic uncertainty alone is and would be intolerable; but imagine if the Brexiteers in the ruling Tory Party refused to countenance a compromise with Brussels (on EU terms) to keep airlines flying, fresh food supplies flowing, and the necessary amounts of insulin and cancer treatment drugs available? Manufacturers would probably have already implemented a mass furlough of workers and suspension of production in the face of the paralysis of just-in-time supply chains. Think back to the warning of Ivan Rogers, quoted in Chapter 5 above, about the UK's total dependence on the EU regulatory regime, and the entirely predictable and rational resistance from the civil service and the private sector to 'reinventing' or 'duplicating', at enormous expense, the vast wheel of existing market regulation and testing.

Under these sorts of pressure, how would our new direct democracy cope? How would Smiley's 'florid man' in that Fleet Street pub in *Tinker, Tailor* deal with this? Would a referendum help, or would it all be too late? In any case, what would the question be on the ballot paper? Would we let the currency, bond and FT250 markets do their worst? How would a parliamentary system hobbled by the weight of social media opinion respond to this sudden and almost unimaginable emergency? Can you see a post-May cabinet of economically delusional Brexiteers successfully rising to the challenge with the calm grit and focused insight of Alastair Darling as dawn broke over the City on the morning of 13 October 2008? Today the billionaire Brexiteer will have 'hedged' himself into safety, while the United Kingdom plunges over the edge of economic uncertainty into political chaos. From this unforgiving vantage point, all Brexiteer talk of 'Project Fear' is at once perverse and meaningless because, when confronted with reality, unlike the Brexiteer fantasist, neither the Remainer nor his God flinches at the truth. Nor will we flinch from the need to act. And so we will act.

## Do not go blindly into this befuddled darkness

Given all this, is it not entirely predictable that one of the clearest, simplest and truest statements of the honest position of the United Kingdom, as it collectively faces up to the stark choice that the Brexiteer insists on inflicting on the rest of us, has come from a Welsh realist: Carwyn Jones AM, until December 2018 the First Minister of Wales? In an unadorned and undeceiving address on our shared plight in June 2018, he clearly and sagely argued that our choice, four nations as one, hangs between a set of potential political gains and a set of potential economic losses.

If we opt for monocultural, sovereign independence, we will lose all or many of the benefits of the past four decades of multicultural, cosmopolitan, free-trading membership of the world's largest single economic market. Or we can continue to enjoy these benefits, which depend on our committed, loyal willingness to maintain open borders, cultural diversity and shared sovereignty in pursuit of the peace, prosperity and collective defence of Europe. Our departure from the European Union could be expedited at a trice if we only admit to ourselves and the rest of Europe that there is an economic price for leaving and a political cost for staying. So choose.

Acknowledge the reality of the thing. No more opportunist hovering – we will have a bit of this, and a bit of that – and no more muddled metaphysical dreaming that reality exists only to serve our often-benighted purposes. In the end, reality will land us, in Matthew Parris's telling fishing analogy, on the hard wood decks of what is. So let us make a final decision that works for us all – or accept the fact that we should go our separate ways and pay the resulting price even if that price includes the dissolution of the United Kingdom itself. So choose. God help us, choose. And then let go of fear, even if that means letting go of each other.

Made in the USA
Middletown, DE
23 November 2019